Odd-Egg Editor

Odd-Egg Editor

by

Kathryn Tucker Windham

UNIVERSITY PRESS OF MISSISSIPPI
Jackson & London

Copyright © 1990
by Kathryn Tucker Windham

Designed by Sally Horne.

The paper in this book meets the guidelines for
permanence and durability of the Committee
on Production Guidelines for Book Longevity
of the Council on Library Resources.

Library of Congress Cataloging-in-Publication Data
Windham, Kathryn Tucker.
   Odd-egg editor / by Kathryn Tucker Windham.
      p.   cm.
   ISBN 1-934110-01-9 (alk. paper) : $16.95
   ISBN -13: 978-1-934-11001-0

   1. Windham, Kathryn Tucker.   2. Journalists—United States—
Biography.   2. Women journalists—United States—Biography.
4. Women in journalism—United States.   5. Alabama—Social life
and customs.   I. Title.
PN4874.W675A3   1990
070'.92—dc20
   [B]   90-12131
                                                    CIP

For Allen Rankin,
who, by going off to fight
in World War II, made it possible
for me to become
Odd-Egg Editor

Odd-Egg Editor

Chapter 1

WHEN I was a little girl in Thomasville, Alabama, my playmates—Evelyn, Teace, Ruth, Eloise, Patsy, Rosamond, Beryl—wanted to grow up to be teachers, nurses, secretaries or missionaries. I wanted to be a newspaper reporter.

I hung around the *Thomasville Times,* the weekly paper my cousin Earl Tucker edited. I learned to set headlines by hand, choosing the letters from the worn wooden type cases and arranging them on the metal stick, and I learned to operate a small foot-pedal press where we printed notices about traveling shows, revival meetings, political rallies and Negro funerals.

Though I never mastered the operation of the Linotype, I miss the rhythmic, metallic clatter of its falling matrices when I visit newspapers now, just as I miss the clicking of the reporters' typewriter keys and the mechanical chatter of teletypes bringing news from far away. Newsrooms today are too silent, depressingly silent, as though their life and excitement departed with the noise.

Earl let me write movie reviews of coming attractions at the local movie theatre (I thus earned a pass to all the picture shows), and he taught me to read columns of metal type upside down from left to right, a skill I later found useful.

I read the exchanges, mostly weekly papers, that accumulated on a long pine table near the press, and occasionally Earl and I would talk about how sorry a particular paper was or what good feature stories other papers carried. Leroy Gates, the Linotype operator, used those exchanges to start fires in the stove in the wintertime.

At home I read the *Montgomery Advertiser:* Grover Hall's editorials, Max Moseley's sports page, and Atticus Mullin's "Passing Throng." That was the paper I wanted to work for.

So, shortly before I graduated from Huntingdon College in Montgomery, I went down to the *Advertiser* to apply for a job.

Hartwell Hatton, the city editor, leaned back in his swivel chair and stared straight at me. Then, never taking his pipe from his mouth, he said, "I've read some of your articles. You write well. If you were a man, I'd hire you. But I don't want any female reporters." He turned back to the clutter of paper on his desk. My first job interview was over.

The time was the spring of 1939, and I needed a job. It had never once occurred to me that the paper I wanted to work for would not want me. Certainly I never expected to be rejected solely because I was a girl!

It was my first encounter with sex discrimination.

So, after my college graduation, still disappointed and stunned by Hatton's rejection, I went back home to Thomasville where I worked with my mother in her insurance agency, frequented my cousin Earl's newspaper office and was a stringer (at ten cents per inch) for the *Mobile Press-Register,* the *Montgomery Advertiser* (Hatton used my stories despite my being a girl!), and the *Birmingham News.*

I wrote about Thomasville's first traffic light; about the coffins that floated out of the basement of Kimbrough's store when the town ditch flooded; about fiddlers' conventions; about Indian artifacts unearthed in an archeological dig; about Clarke County's earliest historian, the Rev. Timothy H. Ball.

The first twenty-five dollars I earned (it took 250 inches of copy to earn twenty-five dollars), I used to buy Ball's *History of Clarke County.* Two elderly sisters in Grove Hill sold me their copy of the book, took it out of the old round-top trunk where it had lain for goodness knows how many years. "I always meant to read it, but I just never did. Papa read it and told me about some of the things in it. I don't believe Papa admired Reverend Ball," one of the sisters told me. The other sister was counting the twenty-five one-dollar bills I had handed her.

Ball's history became the nucleus of my collection of local history and continues to be my most treasured book.

During those months at home, I also wrote about sweet-gum gatherers and ochre mining and quilters and home-comings and the replacement of steam engines with diesel-powered locomotives on the Southern Railroad. Cousin Earl and I rode in the engine of the first diesel to roll into Thomasville, and I had the honor of blowing the whistle. That diesel whistle, though loud, lacked character. I still miss hearing the whistles of steam locomotives.

While I waited for Hatton to "forgive" me for being a

girl, I organized a Girl Scout troop in Thomasville and taught a teen-age Sunday School class at the Methodist Church.

In 1940 I took the census in Thomasville, counted every one of the 1,200 folks there. I was familiar with the streets (though not their names) and alleys of the town, knew where nearly everybody lived. I did not need the map so thoughtfully provided by the U. S. Census Bureau, except in the area of town known as Cogle's Quarters. The rows and rows of unpainted company houses, built with pine lumber from Bruce Cogle's mill, all looked exactly alike, and I would never have been able to complete an accurate enumeration there had I not had the help of Sweetenin'.

Sweetenin', who lived in the quarters with her parents and six or eight siblings, attached herself to me the first afternoon I appeared there. She was about seven years old. "I'll help you," she said simply, as though she understood thoroughly what my mission was and had been awaiting my arrival. She would laugh when I, confused by the unvarying pattern of weathered houses with hard-swept yards, asked, "Haven't we been down this street before?"

"No'm. We ain't been on this row before." And she would run ahead of me, her bare feet stirring up swirls of dust, announcing; "White lady coming to take yo' senses! White lady coming to take yo' senses!" Despite what must have been some hesitancy or apprehension about having their "senses" taken, the residents came out of their houses to meet me on their porches or in their yards.

Sweetenin' would sit on the steps or play with children in the street (my presence attracted a small coterie of followers, but Sweetenin' made it plain that she was my sole authorized assistant) until I finished my questioning and was ready to move to a new location. Again my little herald would run ahead of me with her chorus of, "White lady coming to take yo' senses! White lady coming to take yo' senses!"

Thomasville's 1940 population would likely not have passed the 1,000 mark if Sweetenin' had not helped me "take the senses."

Then one day the telegram from Montgomery came. Allen Rankin, police reporter and feature writer for the *Alabama Journal,* the afternoon paper of the *Montgomery Advertiser* company, was entering military service and the paper needed a replacement. Was I interested? I was!

So in March, 1941, I moved to Montgomery to begin my newspaper career. My salary as a new reporter was $15 a week, not a forty-hour week, but a work week as long as was needed to cover the news. There was no overtime pay, no bonuses. I believe Allen Rankin had been paid $22.50 a week for covering the same beat. He was a man.

The *Alabama Journal* and the *Montgomery Advertiser* were housed in a three-story brick building on the corner of Dexter Avenue and Lawrence Street. The press room was in the basement and business offices were on the first floor. A dark, steep stairwell led from the sidewalk on Lawrence Street up to the newsroom, with its rows of desks and typewriters. Tall windows, recessed to leave deep ledges for stacking papers or for sitting, overlooked Lawrence Street. The editorial offices had a fine view of Dexter Avenue. It was beneath those windows that bands from Tuskegee Institute and Alabama State College used to serenade the

Advertiser's editor, Grover C. Hall, Sr., when those two schools had their annual football clash.

The newsroom was crowded, dingy, stuffy. The move into new quarters, a block away from Dexter at the corner of Lawrence and Washington, was already underway, so no attention had been given the old, deteriorating office in quite some time. The newspaper's owner, R. F. Hudson, did not believe in spending money unnecessarily. Some of his employees referred to him as "Glue Fist" Hudson, but I didn't learn of his nickname, didn't even meet the man, until several weeks after I joined the staff.

My city editor was Meriwether Lewis Sharpley, recently imported from Chicago and said to be tainted by the yellow journalism of that city's press. He must have been around forty years old; his thinning, curly, sandy hair was showing touches of grey; his complexion was ruddy; he was overweight; and he chomped constantly on an unlit cigar, consuming it by bits rather than smoking it. His voice was raspy, and he was atwitch with nervous energy.

"Miss Tucker," he said to me the first morning I reported for work, "Mr. Rankin will take you to the police station and show you what to do. Keep a carbon of every story you write and compare it with the edited version that appears in the paper. I expect you to learn from your mistakes which, I trust, will be few. I will discuss your work with you after the paper comes out every afternoon. Any afternoon you do not see one of your stories on the front page of the *Journal,* do not come back to work the next day. Your desk is right over there."

My desk, swivel chair, and typewriter were scarred by years of hard use. Only my copy paper—stacks of unbleached sheets of newsprint—was fresh, unused.

I knew Allen Rankin (his younger sisters were friends of mine when I attended Huntingdon), and I was aware that he was possibly the best feature writer in the whole state. I never asked him what he thought of my taking over his job as police reporter, and he never told me.

Fact is, Allen didn't give me much instruction or background about the job. I found out later that he was unpopular with the police. His barbed comments about their failures and shortcomings, his exposure of irregularities in the department angered them. In fact, Paul Rapport, the short, rotund, aging chief of detectives, had floored Allen with a quick right to the jaw the week before I arrived. So they were pleased with his departure and would have welcomed any replacement—except a girl. They weren't quite ready for a female to invade their all-male province.

Oh, they were polite enough, the desk sergeants and the detectives. Killing polite, Mother would have said. I sensed their hostility, their unspoken opinion that the police beat was no place for a woman.

Allen did explain to me the difference between the blotter and the docket and showed me how to check the report book. "Their handwriting is sometimes hard to read, and their spelling and grammar are terrible," Allen warned me, speaking softly so that the cluster of policemen nearby would not overhear his remarks. "Some of them are pretty dumb. Maybe most of them.

"You'll like the police court judge. He's a fine fellow, a real country squire," Allen continued as we walked down the tile hall toward the courtroom. We pushed through the double doors, opened the swinging gate in the wooden railing around the judge's bench, and took our seats along the wall where we could see and hear all the proceedings.

From Allen's description, I had expected the judge to be well past middle age, a plump man, possibly with a goatee. I was wrong. Judge John Baytop Scott was in his mid-thirties, handsome, with laughing brown eyes. Instead of the white goatee I had envisioned, he had a clipped brown mustache. Allen made the proper introductions, and Judge Scott said, "Well, so we're to have a lady with us. I hope our manners will improve, that we will be on our best behavior!"

I noticed that morning that Judge Scott seemed to know many of the prisoners and that he listened to what each one had to say. Later, much later, I learned to know the "regulars," the repeaters whose chronic violations of the law brought them often to court.

"We try to dispense basic justice here," Judge Scott said to me after court. "Justice tempered with mercy, and, occasionally, a little laughter. We're all sinners."

So Allen departed for the Air Corps, leaving me to fend for myself at the police station and to cope with Meriwether Lewis Sharpley, as demanding a city editor as ever lived.

When I arrived at work each morning, I'd find a batch of Associated Press and International News Service stories on my typewriter, each one marked "Local Angle." Sharpley believed that every news story somehow affected Montgomery and that local readers needed and wanted to know how the events touched their lives. "Bring it home!" he'd tell me. "Rewrite the story with Montgomery in the lead."

News sources were not always easy to get in touch with early in the morning, but I did the best I could. Around eight o'clock I'd head for the police station, three blocks away, so I'd have time to check the incident reports before court started at eight-thirty. Usually the janitor and the current "floor boys" would be mopping the red tile floors when I arrived, and the place had a damp, soapy, sometimes sour smell.

The desk sergeants would greet me politely, their politeness mixed with curiosity and with their prejudices against female reporters. "Don't you know a police station is no fit place for a nice young lady? What are you doing here? You ought to be writing about weddings and parties and such," they said to me.

"I don't know enough adjectives to be a society editor," I replied. I'm not sure they knew what adjectives are.

They did know how to make my job difficult for me. They "misplaced" reports or "forgot" to tell me about certain gambling raids or robberies.

On one occasion, early in my career, the officers filled out a false report of a large burglary out in Cloverdale, one of Montgomery's fine residential areas. The burglars, the report said, made off with thousands of dollars worth of silver and heirloom jewelry.

In my innocence, I took the report at face value, and wrote a long story about the burglary, complete with quotes from the detectives who were supposedly working on the case. It never occurred to me to check the names of the victims or the address in a city directory. Fact is, I did not know how to use a city directory. I'd never seen one, and neither Allen nor Sharpley had included use of the directory in their basic instructions to me.

But I learned. I learned.

I learned that many police officers bore down hard with a

pencil when they filled out reports. Even if the original report was "misplaced," I could often read it from the imprint left on the blank form that had been beneath it in the pad. The police chief, who always called me "Miss Kathryn," never knew that I could face him at this desk and read all the reports on it while I carried on a conversation with him. Reading those reports upside down was a lot easier than reading newspaper type, a skill I had learned in my cousin Earl's printing office.

I also learned that in nearly every organization there are disgruntled members who will, if they are guaranteed protection, give full and usually accurate accounts of behind-the-scenes shenanigans. I tried to ferret out such sources.

I still had much to learn. Looking back, I am amazed at my innocence—in many areas.

One morning, for instance, as I approached police headquarters, I saw a group of twenty or twenty-five young girls, all stylishly dressed, entering the front door. By the time I got to the desk, they had gone down the hall and were walking down the steps to the basement. "Who are your visitors?" I asked. "Is that a sociology class from the college?"

"Sociology class! Sociology class!" the policemen whooped. "She thinks they're a sociology class from college!" Everybody was laughing.

"Those are prostitutes," one of the policemen finally told me. "They've come to get their monthly blood tests." I'd never seen a prostitute before, not that I knew of. I certainly never thought that a prostitute was as young and attractive as were the girls I had just seen.

After they had stopped laughing at my ignorance, had

eased off on their teasing, a sergeant explained what he called the "facts of life" to me. Prostitution, although it was illegal, was licensed in Montgomery. In small files in the detective department were photographs and records of all the girls who were properly registered. The file contained basic information about each one (name, age, address, police record—if any—and results of her periodic visits to the health department for venereal disease testing), and both Maxwell Field and Gunter Field had duplicate files, helping them to track down any spreaders of venereal disease. Any girl practicing her trade without being registered with the police was subject to arrest on the charge of vagrancy.

Later, after Maxwell and Gunter began rapid expansion, Montgomery's houses of prostitution were closed and the system of registration ended. The girls stopped making their periodic trips to the police station and the health department—but the police never let me forget my innocent mistake.

I do not know how long the teasing, the belittling, the efforts to mislead me, the failure to accept me would have continued if the drownings of two little girls had not occurred.

The girls were sisters, Euline and Juanita Hicks, twelve and ten years old. They left their Martha Street home Monday morning, April 21, 1941, on their way to Cottage Hill School, but apparently they decided not to attend classes that day. They gave their school books to a playmate with instructions for the child to take the books to their teachers and to tell the teachers that they, Euline and Juanita, had to go to the doctor to see if they had chicken pox.

The children's teachers were not alarmed when they failed to report to the school; their attendance was rather irregular. However, their mother became worried when they had not returned home by suppertime, and she notified the police.

The police responded immediately with an intensive search for the sisters. They questioned neighbors, relatives, playmates, everybody who might have seen them between home and school. Nobody could supply any information as to their whereabouts; they had vanished without a trace. This was the kind of story that Sharpley relished. "Cover it," he said to me. "Cover all angles."

I did. I described the clothing the girls were wearing when they disappeared: Euline had on a red-and-white dress with brown-and-white shoes, and Juanita was wearing a green-and-white checked gingham. I quoted sources who feared the pair had been kidnapped, and I wrote about the distraught mother's fear that they had become the victims of a sex fiend. Each day Sharpley gave the story a bigger play, and each day I had to find something sensational to report about the investigation.

Sunday afternoon, almost a full week after the girls' disappearance, I was strolling along a sidewalk near Cloverdale Pharmacy (I had squandered a dime on an ice cream cone), when a police car pulled up beside me. "They've found the girls' bodies in the river," one of the officers told me. "Want to go see?" I got on the back seat, and we headed toward the river.

The body of Juanita had been found Sunday morning by military personnel from Maxwell Field who were searching for an enlisted man who had drowned, the police told me.

Euline's body was found later by fishermen a few miles further downstream. The child's clothing, her red-and-white dress, had snagged on a fence that extended into the water at that point. An empty rowboat was drifting nearby.

The fishermen managed to get the child's body into that boat and tried to return to the Montgomery landing with it, but the boat swamped and they had to take the body back to the area where they had found it. They left the corpse on a strip of sandy beach, beneath a rather high bluff, and headed upstream to notify police that the second body had been located.

"Sure you want to go?" one of the policemen asked. "Those bodies were in the river a long time and they're in bad shape. You probably don't want to see them."

"I want to go," I replied.

We had to park the car and walk across a field and a strip of woods to get to the place where Euline's body lay, and it was almost dusk when we arrived. I forced myself to look at the remains of the little girl, lying at the edge of the muddy water. Flies buzzed around her pale face. The stench drifted up to the bluff where we stood. I coughed and turned away.

The policemen conferred with the boatmen who had tried to retrieve the body, and they all agreed that the remains would have to be brought up the bluff and taken out by ambulance. A stretcher and body bag would be needed. The boatmen headed their craft back upriver, toward Montgomery.

"Well," one of my companions said, "somebody has got to stay here with the body while we go back to Montgomery to get the help and equipment we need. It will be dark soon, and we don't want anything—'possums or such—to eat . . ." He dropped his voice. "Think you can handle the assignment? Should make a good story."

"Sure," I replied. "I can handle it." I was glad there was not light enough for them to see my face.

One of the men handed me a flashlight, the big, heavy-duty kind law enforcement officers use. "Shine this down on her every now and then to frighten animals away. We'll be back as soon as we can." And they were gone.

The darkness closed in on me. I had the night sounds of a raucous katydid chorus, the drone of mosquitoes, and the distant barking of dogs for company. And a little dead girl.

I don't know how long I stood there on that river bluff. An hour? Two hours? It seemed an eternity. Every few minutes I would walk to the edge and focus the flashlight on the body. No predators came, but, though I tried to avoid looking at it, I saw that the body of the child had already been preyed on before it was taken from the water.

Finally the policemen, several of them, returned with stretcher, ropes, and pulleys, all the equipment needed to hoist the body up the river bank and into a waiting am-bulance. I handed the flashlight to an officer, and a patrol car took me home. I did not sleep very well that night.

Next morning I went to work early and told Sharpley about my involvement in the recovery of the bodies. "Write it," he ordered.

So I wrote it. I told of the mother who had kissed her little daughters goodbye when they left for school the day of their disappearance; of the airmen who had found the first body floating in the river, and of the fisherman who had found the other body lodged near the water's edge; of the state of decomposition of the fully-clothed corpses; of the cockleburs tangled in their hair, caught in the new permanent waves their mother had given them; of the inaccessibility of the location where the second body was found; of the difficulty of removing those dead children from the river to a funeral home.

I even wrote of the prostrated grief of the mother when she learned that her daughters were dead; of the two white baptismal dresses hanging limply in the closet (Euline and Juanita were to have been baptised at the Clayton Street Baptist Church the very Sunday night their bodies were removed from the river); of their father, serving time at Kilby Prison on a burglary conviction.

Sharpley leaned over my shoulder. "Write, Miss Tucker! Write!" he shouted each time I paused to think. "Write!" He snatched each paragraph—sometimes each sentence—from my typewriter as I completed it, giving me no opportunity to rewrite or to make any changes whatever in my story. "Write!"

He ran the story with huge headlines, letters an inch and a quarter high (120-point type), all across the top of the front page:

DID HICKS SISTERS DROWN OR WERE THEY MURDERED?

There was little indication that the sisters had been murdered, although the coroner's report did show that there was no water in their lungs, and the presence of cockleburs in their hair was puzzling. The most widely held theory was that they had drifted out into the river in a boat, one they had chanced upon at the city wharf, had fallen overboard and drowned.

Sharpley, as was his nature, wanted to make the story as sensational as possible. The paper ran, along with my story, a four-column picture of the mourning mother lying in bed with a damp cloth across her forehead. School pictures of Juanita and Euline were inset on her flowered bedspread. The pictures, made before they got their permanent waves, showed the girls with straight, shoulder-length hair and laughing eyes.

Cotton middling closed at 11.10 that day, April 28, 1941, and the *Alabama Journal* sold for five cents a copy.

After my story was written, Sharpley sent me out to Kilby Prison to tell the girls' father that his daughters were dead. "I've made arrangements with the warden," he told me. "You go get the story." I still wonder what sort of arrangements were made.

When I arrived at the walled bastion on the outskirts of Montgomery, I was escorted by a guard into the warden's office, and Jack Hicks was brought in. The prison grapevine had already informed him of his daughters' deaths. The prisoner was tall and thin, thirty-five years old but already beginning to stoop, and pale with the pallor of being behind bars for almost a year and a half. "They're really dead—my babies—ain't they?" he asked in a slow, choking voice.

"Yes," I answered. I had wondered what I would say to the man, what words I could use, but it was he who did the talking.

"I just can't quite believe it," he sobbed. "When they'd come to see me on Sundays, they'd tell me about school and about their friends and all, and when I asked them if everything was all right, they told me it was. They seemed happy.

They didn't have no cause to try to run away. But who would want to harm my little girls? Who?" He shook his head and wiped his eyes on the sleeve of his prison jacket.

The warden spoke. "You've been given a three-hour parole to go with a guard to your daughters' funeral tomorrow afternoon," he said.

Jack Hicks was pitifully grateful. "Thank you, sir. Thank you," he kept repeating. As he turned to leave the room, he looked at me and said softly, "My little girls were the only people in the world who loved me."

Sharpley gave that story a good play, too.

After news spread around police headquarters that I had stood guard alone on the dark river bank, the policemen's attitudes toward me slowly changed. They began to accept my presence, to treat me with respect. Oh, they would occasionally ask if the big Cloverdale burglary had been solved, or they would tease me about mistaking prostitutes for college students, but I had proven that I could handle a tough beat "almost as well as a man."

That qualification, "almost as well as a man," did not please me, but I welcomed gratefully the headway I had made.

Chapter 2

MEANTIME, back at the office, I was also making some progress. Sharpley taught me:

1. That a robbery and a burglary are not the same thing.

2. That husbands are survived by widows, not wives.

3. That accident victims who "sustain" injuries do not die.

4. That funeral services are held at, not from, churches or funeral homes.

5. That death is always unexpected and, therefore, the word should never be used in that connection.

6. That few things are more important than the correct spellings of names.

I, having had good English teachers, already knew the difference between "it's" and "its." Misuse of an apostrophe could set Sharpley wild.

He also taught me about posing photographs for newspaper use. One of my early assignments was to cover a convention. I returned to the paper with my story, and the photographer went into the darkroom to develop the picture I planned to use for the illustration. He showed me the glossy print before he handed it to Sharpley. I was pleased; each face in the two rows of sixteen or twenty officers and delegates (they all were delighted to be in the picture) was quite distinct.

"Miss Tucker!" Sharpley called. I walked over to his desk, expecting a word of commendation. He pointed to the picture. "Have all of these people been killed in some terrible accident?"

"No, sir."

"Never have more than five, preferably no more than four, people in a picture unless the entire group has just met a gory or unusual death. Understand?" He threw the photograph into the wastebasket.

Sharpley continued to hover over me while I was typing, particularly if a deadline was approaching, exhorting me to "Write! Write! This is not the Great American Novel you are writing. Tomorrow it will be used on the bottom of a birdcage or will be wrapped around garbage. Write!" And he tore the sentences and paragraphs (I was fortunate if I finished a paragraph) from my typewriter almost as soon as I touched a period. It was what was known, I suppose, as learning to write under pressure.

It was about this time that the title of "Odd-Egg Editor" was conferred upon me. It was Sharpley, in one of his lighter moments, who made the announcement. "As Odd-Egg Editor," he told me, "it will be your duty to interview and to write a story—sometimes with photographs—about anyone who brings a freakish article into the newsroom. Not just eggs. Anything freakish."

So I, as Odd-Egg Editor, wrote about gourds that grew in the shapes of animals, usually rabbits; fish that had swallowed knives, coins and jewelry; okra pods four feet long; fruit trees that blossomed out of season; albino squirrels; triple ears of corn; dogs that could bark "Dixie"; three-legged chickens; sows nursing kittens; tomatoes growing on potato vines and vice versa; twelve-pound turnips; peaches misshapen into the likeness of Winston Churchill; and more such.

I also wrote about odd eggs brought into the newsroom, dozens of them. Most common were those shaped like dumbbells or hourglasses, but after Pearl Harbor there was a proliferation of eggs bearing prophetic messages on their shells, usually in Japanese. Maybe the messages weren't really in Japanese, but I could not decipher what the eggs' owners told me were predictions of victory or defeat or warnings of dire catastrophy. Generally only the owners of the hens that laid the eggs were able to translate the scribblings. The few "messages" I ever saw clearly were distinct *V*'s (obviously *V* for Victory), and there were many of them.

One of the finest of the odd eggs was laid by Mrs. M. T. Law's dominicker hen at Deatsville. The egg had maps of the major Allied countries clearly outlined on its shell. The map of the United States, which was readily recognizable, had a large *V* on its heartland. Maps of England and Russia were marked by smaller *V*'s.

As far as I was ever able to learn, none of those odd eggs was ever eaten. Several egg owners shuddered and grimaced at the mere suggestion of consuming their oddities, indicating that eating them would border on sacrilege. One woman assured me that she intended to keep her egg (it was embossed with what she interpreted as numbers revealing the date World War II would end) right beside her Bible. "My hen was divinely inspired," she told me in a reverent tone.

Not all the odd eggs that found their way into the newsroom were inanimate; some rather unusual human beings came up those stairs, too. Back in the 1940s there was no form of security at most newspaper offices, no guard to pass or register to sign (name—purpose of visit—time in—time out), no tags to wear, so anybody could walk right in—and did.

One of our frequent visitors was Shorty (he must have had a real name, but nobody knew what it was) Peek. Shorty would come breezing into the newsroom, his straw hat in one hand and his briefcase in the other, bowing politely to everyone he passed. Even empty desks merited a bow. Shorty favored white clothing, as befitted one of his innocence. His white linen coat was usually loose and wrinkled, and his white pants barely covered the tops of his socks (also white). His white buck shoes, a size or so too large, slapped smartly against the floor as he headed for the city desk.

"See Miss Tucker—right over there," he was always told. Since I was Odd-Egg Editor, Shorty was one of my people.

After the formality of introductions, which Shorty always insisted upon, he would pull one of his flags out of his briefcase and spread it out on my desk. "Many people do not know the difference between a real flag and a religious flag," Shorty would tell me in a rote tone that indicated he had delivered this explanation many times before. He said slowly, "This flag I drew from a vision I had in the federal prison." He smoothed out the wrinkled paper so I could see the figure of Christ on the cross against a background of red and white stripes and blue stars. Various angels hovered around the central figure, and both a moon and sun vied with the stars for brightness.

"See? This is a religious flag. I would not deface my country's flag. I glorify it!" He would give me the earnest, quizzical look of an artist hoping his imaginative work would be understood. I wish I had kept some of the drawings Shorty brought into the newsroom, wish I could show them to President Bush and ask if he thinks the little man should have been charged with defacing the flag.

Then there was "Bicycle," a scrawny, middle-aged man, whose whole life was focused on making his bicycle the most colorfully beautiful vehicle in the world. His bicycle was one of the old balloon tire models whose make had long been eradicated by modification, additions—and decorations. He had the usual squirrel tails on his "wheel," but those were only the drab beginnings. A line of eight or ten horns was attached to the handlebars, and each of the noise-makers was festooned with flowing ribbons. Pinwheels, gaudy paper flowers, banners, cattails, toy birds on sticks, flags, streamers covered every inch of the bicycle, protruding at all angles, so that when Bicycle pedaled down Dexter Avenue he looked not like a cyclist but like a miniature float in a parade.

Bicycle used to trundle his bike up the stairs and into the

newsroom for us to admire, but when his decorations became more elaborate, he could no longer maneuver the cumbersome two-wheeler up the steps, so he would entreat us to come out on the sidewalk to see his artistic creations. I, as Odd-Egg Editor, was, of course, the one who went.

The unfortunate aspect of Bicycle's hobby was that not all of his decorations belonged to him. He was inclined to "borrow" any bright object that fit into his decorative scheme, and this flaw in his character sometimes got him into trouble with the law.

On those occasions when the police would take him into custody and he had to appear in police court, he always brought his bicycle into court with him. Judge Scott, though he disapproved of thievery, could not help admiring Bicycle's artistic talents, and he always came down from the bench to examine the latest decorative touches. And, though he delivered a strong lecture to Bicycle on the evils of stealing, Judge Scott always reimbursed the complainant for the pretties Bicycle had "borrowed." Bicycle often spoke proudly of ornaments "my good friend, Judge Scott, gave me." His relationship with Bicycle was a part of Judge Scott's philosophy of tempering justice with mercy—and having a few laughs.

Other courtroom relationships did not always work out so well. There was, for instance, the chronic offender who, when he appeared before Judge Scott one Monday morning, pleaded guilty to the charge of public drunkenness. However, he felt the Judge's sentence was too severe, particularly since he and Judge Scott had been acquainted for such a long time. The defendant stood silently, seemingly stunned, for a minute after the sentence was pronounced. Then he looked pleadingly at the judge, and in a voice that was aimed to soften the hardest heart said touchingly, "Judge Scott, you've been like a father to me."

"Well, I made a mess of bringing you up!" retorted the judge.

Then there was the morning when a small black man, known as "Bogus," had a neighbor arrested for stealing his shotgun. The neighbor, when he appeared before Judge Scott, implicated Bogus's girl friend in the theft. Bogus quickly spoke up in the girl's defense. "Judge," he said, "this girl does my cooking and washing and feeds my dogs and takes care of my chickens and things. I don't believe she had nothing to do with stealing my shotgun. And, even if she did, I don't want her punished. She don't need nothing else done to her. I done already shot her and cut her." The judge agreed she'd been punished enough.

On another occasion, Judge Scott had before him a defendant accused of stealing a shoe, just one shoe. "I didn't steal the man's shoe," the defendant said. "Some of us were having a little fun. This fellow"—he pointed to his accuser—"was asleep on the ground, and we thought we would take his shoe off and build a fire at his bare foot. Just sort of scare him. We was just playing."

"A sort of glorified hot foot, wasn't it?" Judge Scott laughed. "But you're not doing it right. What you do is leave the shoe on, put a match between the shoe and sole, and light it. Like this." The judge demonstrated, blowing the match out quickly. "Case dismissed," he added.

At one police court hearing Judge Scott demonstrated his proficiency at shooting spitballs. The case involved two little boys, eight or ten years old, who were sitting out in the family car studying their school lessons and also sharpening their spitball marksmanship. Down the sidewalk came a portly gentleman. The temptation was too great for one of the lads, and he let fly a spitball. His aim was perfect. The gentleman was not pleased. He demanded to know who had fired the missile, and then he slapped the culprit.

This action did not please the child's mother. She swore out a warrant charging the man with assault and battery, and the case ended up in Judge Scott's court.

"Your honor," the defense attorney began, "my client was struck with a spitball. Now a spitball is made by . . ."

"Oh," the judge interrupted, "I am quite familiar with spitballs." He tore off a scrap of paper and fashioned a fine spitball while he listened to the rest of the testimony. Then he laughed and dismissed the case. "It wasn't worth getting so upset about," he told the group. "The boy was probably wrong in shooting the defendant—though he did present a tempting target—and the defendant was probably wrong in punishing the boy. In any event, no harm was done."

He turned to the bailiff. "Got a rubber band?" His request granted, the judge let fly with his spitball. It smacked against the rear wall of the courtroom. "Just wanted to be sure I hadn't forgotten how," he said.

One morning Judge Scott had before him a defendant who was charged with having escaped from police custody. "I understand you were a trusty, a floor boy, here in the police department and that you walked off. Is that right?"

"Yessir, your honor," responded the defendant. "Somebody come by and give me a secret sign that meant it would be good for me if I left. So I left."

"Well," said the judge, "I'm going to give you a sign. Watch." He held up his hands and extended his fingers three times. "My sign meant thirty days," he explained.

It may have been this same trusty who decided he had served long enough, accosted the desk sergeant and requested his discharge papers. The sergeant got a whiff of the trusty's breath and exclaimed, "Why, you've been drinking! We'll have to put you out to work on the street just as soon as I can get you some stripes to put on." At those words, the floor boy keeled over backward and began having what looked like a major fit. He even frothed at the mouth. The nearby police officers hurried to his aid and were about to summon medical assistance. Then they found four pieces of soap in his mouth, enough to produce a convincing froth. Almost.

Not all of the unusual characters I encountered were in police court.

One morning Sharpley said to me, "There's an African prince speaking out at Alabama State. Go interview him." He handed me a slip of paper with an address on it.

I rang the doorbell at an apartment on the edge of the college campus, and presently a tall, very dark man opened the door. He was wearing a bright-patterned, flowing robe and a close-fitting cloth cap with gold embroidery on it. I introduced myself and told him I had come to interview him for the *Alabama Journal*.

"Do you have an appointment? It is not customary for me to receive guests without an appointment." He spoke with a polished British accent, and his bearing was indeed regal. I had never been in the presence of royalty before, and I was embarrassed by my failure, though unintentional, to observe proper protocol. I stammered a jumbled explanation, feeling more and more uncomfortable for having breached royal etiquette.

"Since you are here, you may come in," the prince said.

For half an hour I listened as he talked, not about himself but about his interest in collecting and writing African folk tales. "Those tales are disappearing from our culture. Someone must save them," he explained solemnly. I had no opportunity to ask questions—I'm not sure I would have dared to. The prince rose and nodded toward the door.

"I bid you good day," he said. I left.

It was a humbling experience.

Not from Africa but from South America came Julio Cesar Berrizeitia. This twenty-year-old Boy Scout from Caracas, Venezuela, bounded up the steps to the newsroom one day soon after I started to work for the *Journal*. He was on his way to Washington, D.C., and he calculated he had already walked 19,308 miles.

He spoke no English and I spoke no Spanish, but with the aid of an interpreter, I learned that Julio and his four companions, also Boy Scouts, had set out on their journey on November 1, 1938. They took a circuitous route to avoid meeting with savage Indian tribes who roamed about the interior of Venezuela. Despite these precautions, he said, they encountered Indians on the Venezuela-Columbia border on December 14, 1938. Julia's throat and left shoulder bore scars of wounds he said he received from the arrows of the primitive tribesmen. "We didn't fight—we ran!" Julio said.

He had other scars, a gash above his eye and long, ugly, healed-over injuries on his legs. "Jungle tiger," Julio explained. "I kill him!" He pulled his weapon, a Boy Scout knife, from the top of his boot and demonstrated how he had slain the beast. He was a good actor; no translation was needed. His Scout neckerchief was pulled through a slide of tiger skin, and he wore a tiger skin bracelet on his right arm.

The Scouts got lost in the wilds of Bolivia and were without food or water for many days, Julio's story continued. One of the boys died, and his four companions carried his body 200 miles into Peru for burial. This part of his story, though sad, was confusing to me: I never understood why they were in Bolivia—or even how they got there—on their way to Washington. It was definitely out of the way.

His three remaining companions got homesick and returned to their native land. One of these Scouts made it to Costa Rica before he turned homeward, and one hiked with Julio as far as Mexico, but from there on Julio continued his walk alone. By the time he reached Montgomery, Julio had worn out fifty pairs of boots. He had a guitar with him, but I never found out for sure whether the musical instrument had accompanied him on his entire journey (it would surely have been a hindrance when he was fighting tigers and fleeing from Indians) or whether he acquired it in Montgomery. He played and sang rather well.

I never quite understood either why he felt the urge to walk from Venezuela to Washington, never knew exactly what his mission was. The closest Julio could come to explaining was to say, "I have gift for President Roosevelt. I have brought him a pressed yellow flower from Paraguay."

It seemed a long way to walk to deliver one pressed flower. And Paraguay?

My story about Julio was picked up by the Associated Press, and one of the New York dailies (*not* the *New York Times*) called me for more details. It was the first time I had ever spoken long distance anywhere outside of Alabama, and I remember being surprised at how clearly the New York reporter's voice, though Yankee, could be heard. About a week later I received a ten-dollar check from the New York paper for the information I supplied them. It was the easiest money I had ever made, and it made me mighty glad Julio had found the Odd-Egg Editor.

I hope he got to Washington with his pressed yellow flower.

Chapter 3

IN THE DAYS before Pearl Harbor I was still covering the police beat, still living with Mr. and Mrs. Allen Woodall and their two little boys, Sonny and Buddy, at 28 Cloverdale Park (I paid forty dollars a month for a room with private bath, maid service and two meals a day), and still being paid fifteen dollars a week. I was making small weekly payments on a Schwinn bicycle and an Underwood portable type-writer. They, and a few books, constituted my worldly possessions.

My recreation budget would have been extremely limited and I would likely have been broke most of the time had it not been for my radio movie reviews and the "lamp shade circuit."

Allen Woodall, who was advertising manager for Radio Station WSFA, arranged for me to get passes to all the movie theatres in exchange for doing brief weekly reviews for the station. The experience I had had writing movie reviews for my cousin Earl's weekly paper, back when I was in high school in Thomasville, stood me in good stead.

For the "lamp shade circuit," I wrote fluffy articles about small local businesses, such as specialty shops, tearooms, home furnishings and interior decorating establishments (hence the name "lamp shade circuit") and others. The articles were used on the business review page of the paper, and I was paid $7.50 weekly for my contributions. This work was separate and distinct from my job as a reporter and was done during my off hours.

Even with my augmented income, I might have gone hungry at noon occasionally if it had not been for Chris's hot dog stand. Chris's place was on Dexter Avenue, convenient to the newspaper office, and until the war with its blackout regulations came along, his big neon sign "Famous Hot Dogs" illumined the area at night. I patronized Chris's nearly every day. At the entrance were racks of cigarettes and candy, often scantily filled because of World War II rationing, and a soft drink box.

Although I cannot now find anyone who can verify it (as Mark Twain said, "I find that the further back I go, the better I remember things, whether they happened or not"), I recall that near the entrance was a device known as a Pan-o-ram where customers could insert a dime and see a talking movie. The machine was a sort of glorified nickelodeon and was owned or promoted by James Roosevelt, son of the president. It obviously was never widely popular, and the advent of television marked its doom.

A long counter with stools extended down the left side of Chris's place, and over on the right side, behind a partition, was a long corridor with booths and small tables along the walls. The stand was crowded with customers (white only) during the lunch hour, and Chris seemed to be everywhere—taking orders, serving food, running the cash register, checking on the kitchen, greeting customers. "Yes, ma'm. Wutkinidufuhyse today, ma'm? One hot dog? Two? Bestindewholewol." They were.

Chris's hot dogs were juicy and tender, served hot on a fresh bun with everything on them, including his own secret Greek sauce. They cost eight cents each. He had to sell a lot of hot dogs to support his wife and five children.

Chris, who had come over from the old country, had a rounding stomach and a swarthy complexion that made him look as if he needed a shave. He had a scattering of gold teeth and his black eyes sparkled with friendliness. He always cashed my check on payday. "Gotta check? How much, ma'm? What? No grow! No grow!" Sometimes I felt that he lamented the smallness of my salary as much as I did.

Chris was intensely patriotic, and after the war started, he was always eager for news. When I walked in, his daily greeting was, "Watzewarnuz? Good? Bad? Wewhipem yet!"

After Pearl Harbor, Chris became even more ardently patriotic. He invested in war bonds and urged his patrons to do the same, he promoted scrap metal and aluminum drives, and he displayed flags all around his hot dog stand. When customers complained of shortages, Chris was prompt to remind them, "Wegottawinwar!"

I was late learning about the attack on Pearl Harbor. That December weekend I had gone to Thomasville to visit my family. I slept late that fateful Sunday morning, waking up in time to join Mother, Aunt Bet and Tabb (Aunt Bet's daughter) for a leisurely breakfast of Tramp Eggs, hot muffins, and fig preserves.

Mother went to teach her Sunday School class at the Methodist Church while I finished baking a batch of Toll House cookies and toasting pecans to take back to Montgomery with me. We all joined Mother at church where we heard our young minister, Conrad Myrick (he later transferred to the Episcopal ministry) discuss the life of Saint Paul. There were the usual after-church greetings and conversations.

After a dinner featuring Mother's smothered chicken (I have never been able to cook it, make it taste as good, as she did), we loaded into Tabb's car and drove to Selma, sixty-five miles away, so I could catch the 4:40 P.M. bus back to Montgomery. We had been too busy and too happy over being together to listen to the radio at home, and Tabb had no radio in her car, so our hours of peace were prolonged.

The bus was nearly to Montgomery when the elderly man sitting beside me spoke of the Japanese attack. I thought—hoped—he was confused or mistaken.

I heard the whole story when I reached the Woodalls' home. They had several guests, among them a young paratrooper officer from Ft. Benning, Georgia, who was excited and eager to return to his base.

Somebody opened a bottle of champagne. "What shall we drink to?" Allan Woodall asked. "To our country? To a quick victory? To the annihilation of Japan?"

"To all of that—and to us. May we meet again soon!" the paratrooper responded. He gulped his glass of champagne and hurried out the door. "Goodbye!" he called back to us. "I'll bring you a souvenir from Japan!"

Later Stan Tarilton, a photographer for the paper, and I went over to Sara Crist's home for a waffle supper. Stan would, months later, be a combat photographer in the Pacific Theatre, photographing some of the places we heard about in radio newscasts that night.

Other friends joined us, including several British cadets who were being trained as pilots at Maxwell Field. We sat in a semi-circle around the radio, some in chairs and others on the floor, as we listened to the newscasts and tried to imagine the scene at Pearl Harbor. Nobody went near the record player, though good music had always been a part of Sara's parties. The waffles got cold.

"We won't be able to put on a skit about Pearl Harbor; it's bigger than even our amazing talents can handle," one of the men commented.

"Shshsh. They're about to give new casualty figures," Horace Perry said. Horace was on the photographic staff at the paper. He could carry amazing sets of figures around in his head and quote them without error days later.

Except for the weary voices of the commentators, we had a silent party at Sara's that night. Even laughter, a traditional guest at our gatherings, was absent.

Next morning Sharpley sent Horace Perry and me out to the city waterworks. "I want you to get a picture showing how easy it would be for the Japs to poison Montgomery's water supply," he said. "Hurry!"

Horace and I did hurry out to Montgomery's unguarded water reservoirs on North Court Street. Horace climbed up on one of the low, round storage tanks and lifted the manhole cover. I photographed him peering down into the city's drinking water. It was the first picture I ever made as a newspaper reporter.

Sharpley ran the picture, three-column size, on page one, together with my story about how Axis sympathizers could wipe out a large portion of the population of Montgomery by dropping either poison or deadly disease germs into the unprotected reservoirs. I pointed out that some of the highest ranking city, state, and county officials drank water from those reservoirs.

That picture and story did not set well at all with Colonel (World War I) William P. Screws, Montgomery's public safety commissioner. I had already had some minor difficulties with Commissioner Screws; unlike most members of his police department, he still opposed my assignment as police reporter. He also became upset because I seldom took notes on events I was covering.

Back when I was in high school, when I already knew that I wanted to be a newspaper reporter, I read in one of New York columnist O. O. McIntyre's columns that a good interviewer never takes notes. A good interviewer looks, listens, and remembers, he wrote, pointing out that mastering the skill of remembering conversations verbatim takes practice but is well worth the effort.

So I began practicing. I would listen to people talking to each other—or to me—and try to recall every word that was said. I even tried to remember our Methodist preacher's sermons every Sunday, but I soon wearied of that exercise. It was more entertaining to watch the members of the congregation and try to recall the stories I had heard about each one of them.

By the time I entered Huntingdon College, a small Methodist-supported liberal arts college in Montgomery, I had become fairly proficient at listening and remembering. I did have to take notes in class (my remembering was the short-term type, did not extend to six-week tests or final exams), but I never needed a pencil and paper when I did interviews for the college newspaper, *The Huntress* (Huntingdon was an all-girl school then).

For some reason, it made Colonel Screws uneasy for me to sit and listen during conferences, meetings, or interviews. He never accused me of errors in my reporting, but he considered it unnatural for reporters not to take notes. He disliked it. It was one of several things he disliked about me.

The colonel/commissioner was also irked on another occasion when I photographed and wrote about piles of aluminum pots and pans, all donated by patriotic citizens to a widely publicized scrap drive, lying on a secluded lot owned by the city. Some 7,000 pounds of aluminum, collected to "Keep 'Em Flying," had become a breeding place for rats and mosquitoes while it awaited shipment to smelters. Commissioner Screws was not directly responsible for the delay in getting the discarded utensils on their way to becoming airplane parts, but he was offended by the story, deemed it unpatriotic. And said so!

Commissioner Screws was not the only official I was having trouble with. Brig. Gen. George E. Stratemeyer, Commanding Officer of the Southeast Air Corps Training Center at Maxwell Field, ordered me banned from the base. He sent his public information officer, a pompous fellow named Capt. Danny Duvall, down to the newsroom to make the announcement. An interview I had done with the general had displeased him. I was not accused of misquoting him; I just should not have quoted him so precisely in print. That was my offense.

The military was not my beat, but Sharpley had sent me out to Maxwell to interview General Stratemeyer soon after his arrival in late January, 1942. The general was handsome, tall and trim, his dark hair touched with grey around the temples, and his mustache clipped with military precision. He reminded me of Errol Flynn, and I said so in my story. That flattery did not displease him. We had a pleasant visit in his office (as I recall, Captain Duvall was lurking in the background) during which he told me that he had been flying since 1916 but that he did not fly overseas during World War I.

"I was either too good or too sorry," he laughed. "They kept me in Texas as an instructor." Then he became serious. "That's a mistake we're making again. We're keeping the best men for instructors instead of sending them out for combat duty." That was the quote that angered him. Maybe he shouldn't have said it, but he did. Having his words in print caused him great distress, so he barred me from Maxwell.

The general had high rank and lots of authority, but there was one part of the base over which he had no control, and I was welcome there. The military was still racially segregated then. On the back side of sprawling Maxwell Field was the headquarters of the Fourth Aviation Squadron, Maxwell's Negro troops. The unit was commanded by Maj. Dwight Wilhelm, a white southerner, who shared my dislike and disdain for Captain Duvall. Except for his own troops, whom he admired and respected, Major Wilhelm did not care much for anything military.

When he learned of my difficulties with Maxwell authorities, he immediately dispatched a courier to invite me out to watch his troops on parade. His command was separate from the rest of the base, and he was in complete charge of all activities there. Of course I accepted his kind invitation.

It gave me a certain satisfaction to enter the main gate at Maxwell, inform the guard that I was a guest of Major Wilhelm, and drive right past General Stratemeyer's headquarters. Going through the back entrance might have been more convenient, but I kept hoping to have an encounter with Captain Duvall or General Stratemeyer if I came in the front way. Major Wilhelm invited me out to Maxwell often, and he usually managed to let word get to Captain Duvall that I was coming or had been there.

On one of my visits I had the opportunity of hearing a group of marching men sing Allen Rankin's "Song of The Bombardiers." Allen, by then, had washed out of pilot training and had been assigned to public relations. Perhaps in line of duty or more likely because he just wanted to, he wrote this song for the bombardiers:

We'll go to hell and tell the Devil, "Hello" for you.
We'll go to hell and put on a very good show for you.
The boys who live to old and grey
Are fighting this war the easy way,
But we'll go to hell and tell the Devil, "Hello."

We'll go to hell and tell the Devil a thing or two.
There'll be plenty of devilettes there who will dance
    and will sing for you.

The wine is good and the beer is free,
And the general is not a bit better than we,
So we'll go to hell and tell the Devil, "Hello."

The marching men seemed to like the song.

In addition to Commissioner Screws and General Strate-meyer, I had another enemy, a man whose name I never knew. He came up the steps and into the newsroom one morning, strode over to my desk and spat out, "So you're Kathryn Tucker! I've been looking everywhere for the re-porter who wrote all those damn lies!"

I was surprised by his attack, but when he then insinuated that I had been "paid off" to write the offensive (to him) article, I was furious. I picked up a Coca-Cola bottle on my desk and rose from my chair. If he had not beat a hasty retreat, I know I would have brained him. My anger fright-ened me: I had wanted to kill the man. I was still young and very idealistic, and the idea that someone thought I could be bribed to write a story infuriated me. I cried, as I always do when I'm angry.

The article in question dealt with the growing problem of delinquent young girls in Montgomery. I rode with the police vice squad one Saturday night and wrote an account of what we saw.

"You see them downtown on Dexter Avenue too late at night, these thirteen-, fourteen-, fifteen- and sixteen-year-old girls," I wrote. "You see them on Wednesday and Satur-day nights at the public dance hall on Dexter where, for the price of a quarter, an unattached soldier or civilian can climb the worn stairs, pick him out a likely-looking girl, maybe dance a little to the music of the juke box or the hillbilly band, and then see how his girl would like to go outside for a breath of fresh air. It's one of those come-and-go places, a lot of coming and going." I later learned that my angry visitor operated the dance hall I had written about.

I wrote about how easy it was for those young girls to get beer or whiskey, and I told about seeing them further downtown, waiting in hotel lobbies while their escorts registered for a room. "Maybe you notice that they're nervous and a little embarrassed. Mostly you notice how young they are," the article said. I quoted law enforcement officers as saying they believed that seventy percent of the illicit sexual relations in Montgomery involved girls sixteen and under.

The article was reprinted in its entirety in *Alabama Social Welfare,* published by the State Department of Public Welfare. I had become an instant authority on juvenile delinquency. Invitations to speak on the subject and to serve on committees and panels began to arrive. I had the good sense to decline them all, and for the first time I became leery of experts and authorities: I knew personally how little real knowledge it sometimes takes to become one.

The problem with young girls becoming prostitutes was serious and increasing in wartime Montgomery. After the licensed houses had been closed and the registration system at police headquarters had been abandoned, the police waged a constant struggle to keep the prostitutes from plying their profession around town. Almost every Monday morning, groups of the girls appeared before Judge Scott in police court. The charge against them was vagrancy. They were arrested loitering around hotel lobbies, at honky-tonks on the edge of town, at what were then called tourist camps, and near the entrances to the military bases especially on pay days.

The first of the sweeping raids by police came in August, 1942, when eleven young white women were taken into custody. In announcing the arrests, Police Chief Ralph King stated, "The War Department has asked us to see that prostitution is stamped out in this city, and we are going to do it!" Support for the war effort took many forms.

The standard punishment for vagrancy meted out by Judge Scott was three months at hard labor. Occasionally he would fine a girl twenty-five dollars plus court costs and order her to leave town. Every now and then he would whisper to me before court, "Kathryn, please go talk to those girls. They're just children! Tell them to go home—I'll get the money for bus tickets."

They were children, some of them, frightened, confused children from small towns and rural areas all across Alabama. Sometimes they cried, sobbing out stories of mistreatment at home or abandonment by boy friends or the lure of easy money. Most of them accepted gratefully Judge Scott's offer to drop charges and to provide transportation home. The judge was not always lenient; repeaters received the maximum sentences, plus scathing lectures.

As a part of the crackdown on prostitution, several tourist camps were closed by officers on the grounds that their premises were being used for "the purpose of a bawdy house, a house of prostitution or a house of ill fame."

Chapter 4

IT WAS AFTER a raid on one of those tourist camps that I first met Billie Jean. She was brought into the courtroom with several women who had been arrested in the raid, but I noticed that she segregated herself from the group, as though she did not want to be closely associated with them.

I could not help noticing her. She looked a little older and a little tougher than her fellow prisoners; looked wiser, too. Her blonde hair was closely cropped, and she wore no make-up. She carried herself with a touch of arrogance and pride that made her seem taller than she was. Police records listed her as four feet eleven inches tall. Those same records described her build as "good," an honest assessment.

She and Judge Scott nodded and smiled at each other. "Well, Billie Jean, looks like you're in trouble again," the judge said.

"Yes, sir," she replied, looking straight at him.

"You're charged with defacing and destroying private property. Guilty or not guilty?"

"The police say I broke out a window at Webber's store, but I don't remember doing it. First thing I remember was waking up in jail," she replied.

"Since you can't recall destroying private property, I'll change the charge to vagrancy and sentence you to six months in the state prison." Billie Jean smiled.

As she left the police station on her way to prison, the policemen waved and called a farewell to her. "See you in six months!"

"Not if I see you first!" she called back over her shoulder.

After court, my first question to Judge Scott was, "Who is that woman?"

"Some people call her the Blonde Bombshell, which is a rather apt description of her, and she is also referred to as the Bloodhound Tamer. Quite a character!" he began. "I have just sentenced her to her ninth prison term. Her arrest record is longer than she is tall." So Judge Scott told me a bit about Billie Jean, policemen added more stories, and Billie Jean herself eventually talked to me about her past. Some of it, that is.

Whenever her name was mentioned, the bloodhound story was told. Back in 1938, the story goes, Billie Jean was serving a six-month sentence for vagrancy. She wearied of prison life. The brick walls of the century-old prison depressed her. And besides, the way she figured, she had served enough of her sentence. She was ready to leave that place. She knew the punishment for escaping—or attempting to escape—was two weeks in the dark confines of the dog house with a diet of bread and water, but she didn't aim to get caught.

One afternoon she slipped away from the work gang in the prison field, dived into the Coosa River that ran along its edge, and swam across that swift stream. She had hardly reached the other side of the river, hadn't nearly had time to dry off or get her bearings, before the warden sent the bloodhounds after her. The two dogs, noted for their tracking skills and for their viciousness, picked up her trail immediately and ran yelping through the woods. They ran so fast the handlers couldn't keep up with them, but the men figured that was all right, figured it was a good sign they'd have the prisoner back in custody in record time.

Then the yelping stopped. There wasn't a sound, not even a whine, from the hounds. The handlers called and whistled, but the dogs didn't come back. The men searched until dark, calling and whistling, but they found no trace of the bloodhounds. Or of Billie Jean.

The warden wasn't happy, not at all happy, when he heard the report from the dog handlers, but they all expected to see the trackers back at their pens by breakfast time. They were wrong. The dogs did not return. They had vanished. So had Billie Jean.

Several weeks later a Montgomery policeman on routine patrol in the northern part of town happened to glance up on a front porch where he saw Billie Jean relaxing in a rocking chair. The two bloodhounds were lying peacefully at her feet.

It seemed a pity to disturb the tranquil trio, but he did. "They won't bite," Billie Jean assured the officer when he hesitated to come up on the porch. She had completely tamed those bloodhounds.

Billie Jean liked to tell that story (she loved those dogs), but she didn't like to talk about the punishment she received when she was returned to prison.

That wasn't the only time Billie Jean escaped. Soon after women prisoners were moved from the antiquated Wetumpka stockade, known as The Walls, to the modern Julia Tutwiler Prison, a mile or so up the highway, Billie Jean evaded the male guards one night, climbed a fifteen-foot fence surrounding the prison, and escaped into the darkness.

She was serving her eleventh prison term, having been sentenced to 208 days on a charge of vagrancy in Jefferson County. Once again, Billie Jean, although she had served only about a month of the sentence, decided she had been imprisoned long enough, that her offense really did not merit such prolonged punishment—so she left. Billie Jean had a strong sense of fairness. It could have been a mere coincidence that her escape came on the first night that a new acting warden, a man, took over his duties at Tutwiler Prison. Billie Jean was known to favor a woman for the job.

If she had had a different background, Billie Jean herself would have made a good warden at Tutwiler. She was smart, intensely loyal, trustworthy, knowledgeable about the penal system, and a natural leader. The wardens and assistant wardens at Tutwiler recognized and, for the most part, appreciated Billie Jean's leadership qualities. Although she was usually the smallest of the inmates, the other women, black and white, respected her and did what she told them to do. Giving orders came easier to her than taking them.

"Things run easier when Billie Jean is here," a prison administrator once commented. "The barracks are neater, the work goes smoother, there's less fussing and fighting. Most of the inmates stand in awe of Billie Jean—they certainly don't want to make her mad!"

Billie Jean did have a terrible temper. Her temper and her drinking were what kept her in trouble with the law most of the time. When she was angry and drunk, she would fight anybody, take on five or six opponents at a time, some of whom did not know why or whom they were fighting.

When she was drinking, she liked to break glass. That first morning I saw her in police court, she told Judge Scott she did not remember breaking the plate glass window at Webber's department store (she threw one of her shoes through it), but the arresting officers didn't believe her. She was about to throw her other shoe through a second window when the officers arrived on the scene, they said. Months later she confessed to me that she broke the window because the store had sold her a defective pair of shoes ("They started falling apart the first time I wore them") and refused to give her any refund. So she just gave the shoes back to them, right through the front window.

On one of her early visits to Montgomery's new city jail, Billie Jean broke out fifteen window panes before officers could subdue her.

She pretty well tore up everything in a room at a tourist camp one night during a fight with an Air Corps sergeant. When police arrived to quell the disturbance, the sergeant turned on them. That was a mistake. Billie Jean flew into him, screaming, "Don't you ever hit a policeman! They're my friends!" It took four of her friends to rescue the battered sergeant from her wrath.

The policemen may have been, in truth, Billie Jean's best friends, even if they did have to take her into custody often. If her offense was a minor one, the police would often release her with instructions to report to court the following morning. Promptly at 8:25 A.M. Billie Jean would come striding through the swinging doors into the courtroom, grin at the arresting officers, nod politely to the judge, and take her place with the other prisoners awaiting trial.

When her case was called, she would stand before the judge and listen intently to the charge—or charges—against her. If she believed she had transgressed the law, she would plead guilty. "I don't need a lawyer," she used to say. "I've been in more courtrooms than most lawyers I know. And anyhow, the judge and I trust each other."

As for her background, nobody knew for certain anything about her family or her growing-up years, or even where she was born. Her accent was pure southern, but sometimes she would claim to have been born in some far-off, exotic place, and there were at least a dozen towns scattered around Alabama that Billie Jean claimed as her birthplace. She liked variety.

Even her name was subject to change. Early arrest records, dating back to 1932 (she was seventeen years old then), list her name as Hattie Mae. Somehow Billie Jean suited her better. Her last name was variable, too. Usually it was Guthrie, but sometimes it was Wright, and toward the end of her career, she signed in as B. J. Butts.

She told me once that her parents had been Salvation

Army officers and that she played the tambourine in their mission band. Then a no-good man came along and lured her into a life of sin. It was a good story, but I'm not sure how true it was.

Billie Jean and I used to plan to write a book about her life. I wish we had.

In the spring of 1943, after she was released from prison, Billie Jean announced that she was leaving Alabama, leaving her sordid past behind her and going to live a new and wholesome life in Chicago.

"I'm not ever going to see the inside of a prison again. You have too much time to think in prison. I don't like to think," she told me. "At night behind those bars it gets real quiet, and the dark closes in on you and smothers you with memories you're trying to forget. Those long nights torture me—"

There were some tearful goodbyes down at the police station and at a couple of honky-tonks when Billie Jean left. She said she'd write, but nobody ever got even a post card from her.

Several months later, I got a call from the desk sergeant at police headquarters telling me that Billie Jean was dead. The police department had received a telegram from Chicago with the sad announcement and with the request that funds be wired as soon as possible so that her body could be brought back to Montgomery for burial. It was her dying request to be buried in Montgomery with policemen serving as her pallbearers. The desk sergeant wanted to know if I'd contribute to the fund. I did and so did other employees at the newspaper.

After I had taken our money around to police headquarters, I came back to the office and wrote Billie Jean's obituary. It was the finest obituary I ever wrote. My tears were all over it.

Then three days later, Billie Jean came bouncing up the stairs to the newsroom, alive and grinning. "I got homesick," she said. "Thanks for helping me get back to Montgomery."

I lost track of Billie Jean after I moved up to Birmingham. Years later, while doing research in the Alabama Department of Archives and History, I came across an account of her death. This time it was for real.

The news story in the Montgomery *Advertiser,* dated April 21, 1976, attributed her death to "heart trouble, pneumonia, malnutrition, and other ills spurred on by daily liquor consumption." Reporter Kelly Dowe, who wrote the obituary, told of Billie Jean's lengthy arrest record, of her several marriages ("Two of them were legal—the other five were just shack jobs," he quoted her as saying), and, of course, the famous bloodhounds escapade.

Dowe wrote, too, of Billie Jean's shooting one of her husbands (whether or not he was a legal husband was not made clear) in the chest. Immediately after she pulled the trigger, she called police headquarters and said, "Come on up here and bring your dead wagon and get this s.o.b. out of my kitchen!" Billie Jean said she never felt the least bit guilty about that shooting.

It may have been when she was on trial for that death that another classic Billie Jean story evolved. Circuit Judge William Thetford, the story goes, had to halt her trial so that arrangements could be made to get her character witnesses out of jail.

Billie Jean's real obituary had a three-column headline, and the *Advertiser* ran two pictures of her right above the story. Billie Jean would have liked that; she always knew she was good copy.

Chapter 5

BILLIE JEAN made news by breaking out of prison, but there were other women who made news by asking to be returned to the confines of the penal institution. I wrote about at least two women who, after their release from prison, begged to be sent back. Sharpley liked such stories very much.

Mrs. Emma Marshall was seventy-five years old when she was granted a permanent parole from prison. After she had served thirteen years of a life sentence for murdering her husband, the parole board decreed that she could go free. Mrs. Marshall told her prison friends farewell and went to Staten Island to live with her niece.

Before many months had passed, Gov. Frank Dixon began receiving letters from Mrs. Marshall begging him to let her come back to the Wetumpka prison. "It's only a penitentiary, but it is a peaceful home to me," she wrote the governor. "I want to come back to live, die and be buried there." Nobody could believe that Mrs. Marshall really wanted to return to prison, but the letters continued to come.

The people on Staten Island were strange, she wrote, not friendly. The weather was disagreeable. Her days lacked the regimentation and discipline she had been accustomed to. She missed the girls in her Sunday School class. She was miserably insecure without the routine of prison life and the sheltering protection of the thick brick walls. For more than a year the letters came, and then Mrs. Marshall herself came to appear before the Pardon and Parole Board and ask that her parole be revoked.

There were technicalities to be dealt with, but arrangements were made for her to return to her familiar surroundings. Hers was not a poverty case: she handed $135 to the warden with the request that he keep it for her. Her trunk, which she had the faith and foresight to bring with her, contained more cash. She returned to prison because she wanted to.

What she wanted most of all was to attend her Sunday School class, to be again with the girls who called her "Penitentiary Angel," "Peacemaker," "Queen of the Cells." Sharpley sent me out to cover that Sunday School class's session. It was probably the only time ever that a Sunday School class of thirty-five members with a volunteer teacher merited newspaper coverage. There was no mention of overtime pay for me, but I went.

The class met in makeshift quarters in the prison dining hall, a dark, drab place. A chorus of welcomes greeted Mrs. Marshall, and she smiled. The rims of her thick glasses cut into her pudgy cheeks when she smiled, but she smiled often. An attentive girl with dark hair helped her find a comfortable seat, and a young blonde shared a hymnal with her. She didn't really need a hymnal: she knew all the words of the beloved songs. She listened with interest to the teacher and nodded in agreement with some of her statements. When the class ended, she sighed peacefully and said, "It's good to be back. People are so kind to me. And this is home." Then she read the Twenty-third Psalm aloud to the group.

She did not want to talk about her murder conviction, saying she did not like to think about such things on the Sabbath. She did assure me, however, that she was not guilty of killing her husband.

The other returnee was a younger woman, a woman just turned fifty. Unlike Mrs. Marshall, she wanted to return to prison not for life but just for the winter months. Her name was Edna Earl. When she appeared before Judge Scott in police court, she implored him, "Please send me back to prison in Wetumpka."

Arresting officers said they took Edna Earl into custody at the county jail where she had gone to ask to be returned to prison. She was drunk at the time, they said. "We just put her in jail so she could sober up over the weekend," the policemen testified (testimony in Judge Scott's court was always informal). "We thought she'd change her mind about Wetumpka, but it looks like she hasn't."

They were right. Even cold sober, Edna Earl wanted to be sentenced to serve time at the state prison. She had no special attachment to the place, although she had served five terms on vagrancy charges. She just needed somewhere to spend the winter. It was early November, 1942, and the weather was already getting chilly.

"I don't have any home," she told Judge Scott, "no family or folks to take care of me. I figured it out, and if I get sentenced for six months, the weather will be warm when I get out, and then maybe I can make it. I can't take care of myself during cold weather. Judge, please send me back."

Judge Scott was silent for a few moments. "It does seem," he said to her, "that society could do better for you than to send you back to prison. However, if that's what you want, I'll see what can be done for you."

Three days later, after he had had time to investigate the case, the judge did comply with her request and sentence her to six months in the women's prison. Edna Earl laughed aloud and clapped her hands.

As I said, Sharpley liked prison stories.

One of my early assignments was to go out to Kilby to witness release of a prisoner who had served eleven years for a crime he did not commit. His name was Andrew Sanders.

He was a black man (back in the 1940s the newspaper always identified a black person as a Negro—lack of such identification in a news story indicated the person was white) from Bibb County who had been sentenced to die in the electric chair for a criminal attack (we did not use the word rape) on a feeble-minded fourteen-year-old white girl.

Throughout his trial and during his entire prison term the man proclaimed his innocence. His mother, back in Brent, believed he was innocent, and his wife, Mandy Lou, never doubted that he would return to her. Mandy Lou and Andrew had been married two and a half years at the time he was sent to prison, and they had a little boy, one year old. Andrew saw his wife and son once each year when the two of them made the trip from Centreville to Kilby to visit him.

For the first eleven months that Andrew was in prison, he was on death row awaiting execution in the state's electric chair. During all those months, Andrew never stopped hoping that truth would prevail and his life would be spared.

Benjamin Meek Miller, of Camden, was governor of Alabama then (1931), and when Andrew's routine clemency hearing was held, Governor Miller commuted his sentence to life in prison. Andrew moved off death row into the routine of prison life.

In 1940 Andrew applied to the State Board of Pardons and Paroles for a pardon. The man whose testimony had sent him to prison had died in 1933. Although his accuser had made no dramatic death bed confession of the wrong he had done his former employee, Andrew hoped the board would review his case and find him innocent.

The board did review the case, sent an investigator to Bibb County to gather facts. His investigation disclosed that Andrew had indeed been framed. "Investigation discloses the negro was framed by an elderly former employer long engaged in bootlegging and other illegal activities from which he had accumulated a very sizeable estate. This employer, now dead, was, according to law enforcement officers and other reputable, trustworthy citizens, such type character as would not hesitate, for revenge, to do just what was done, i.e., falsify the facts and secure conviction," the report said.

So Andrew Sanders was given a full pardon. I was there at Kilby in Warden Earl Wilson's office when Andrew got the good news. He came in the office to deliver a suit he had pressed for the warden. As he turned to leave, Wilson said to him, "Andrew, wait a minute. I've got some good news for you. You've been pardoned. You can go back home."

A smile spread over Andrew's face. "Lawdy, boss, sho' 'nuff? I can go free? I couldn't never have been treated any better than I was here, but I sho' will be glad to get home!"

So at four o'clock that afternoon the gates of Kilby Prison opened for Andrew Sanders and closed behind him for the last time. He was wearing a new suit, one of the "go free" suits made by women in the Wetumpka prison, and in his pocket was $21.90. The money was to pay for his train fare and traveling expenses to Centreville, plus funds given to each released prisoner based on the amount of time served.

There was no compensation for the 3,862 days Andrew Sanders spent in prison for a crime he did not commit. But he was a free man, going home to Mandy Lou and their son.

Looking back, it seems that I covered a lot of prison stories, both from Kilby Prison where male prisoners were housed and from the women's prison. My stories ranged from accounts of smuggling narcotics into Kilby to a feature on a beauty parlor for the women's prison.

I'll always be grateful that I was never asked to cover an execution. I listened to veteran reporters, older men, tell of watching—and smelling—a man die in the electric chair, and I knew I could not have covered such a story. I did not even like to hear about them.

Some of my prison stories reflected the improvement being made in the treatment of prisoners, particularly women.

My first visit to the women's prison (Julia Tutwiler Prison) at Wetumpka was in June, 1941, when Sharpley sent me out to do a story about the new beauty parlor there. For the first time in history, Alabama women prisoners had a beauty parlor, one with the latest equipment and furnishings. Actually, there were two beauty parlors, exactly alike, one for white prisoners and one for colored.

It had long been the Saturday afternoon custom for the women, those who still cared about their appearance, to shampoo and set each other's hair. Some of them paid to have their hair done, making the payment out of the fifteen-cent weekly allowance each prisoner received. In the new beauty shop, the services were free. A volunteer from Fort Payne spent three days teaching four white prisoners and four Negro prisoners how to use the equipment and how to set hair in styles most becoming to their customers. These eight operators were expected to train other prisoners, creating a continuous training and rehabilitation program.

The state provided the building, its newness contrasting sharply with the 103-year-old brick walls in whose shadow it stood, and paid for all the equipment and supplies, and the inmates did the decorating. They made white tasselled curtains from cotton grown on the prison farm and woven in the prison mill. The lamp shades were fashioned from coat hanger frames covered with osnaburg and appliqued with flowers.

I watched the fledgling beauticians give shampoos and roll hair on curlers, and I tried to help an inmate decide which shade of polish she should use on her newly manicured nails. "I never had a manicure before in my whole life," she said. "I almost feel like a lady!" That was one of the reasons prison officials put the beauty parlor inside those thick walls.

My story and the pictures Horace Perry took (I don't recall that we ever asked any inmate if she objected to having her picture printed in the newspaper, and, though we did not use names, we showed most of the women full face) were good, I thought, but I objected to the headline: GAL IN CELL 13 WANTS MARCEL! Male patrons of the barber shop at Kilby Prison were never so belittled.

I went with E. P. Russell in late March, 1943, when he paid an informal visit to Tutwiler Prison. Russell had recently been appointed Director of the Department of Corrections and Institutions by Gov. Chauncey Sparks, and he wanted first-hand knowledge of how the prison was being run, wanted to "look the situation over," as he said.

A softball game was in progress in the prison yard when we arrived. Russell stood behind a cluster of spectators and watched the game for several minutes. His presence might have gone unnoticed if he had not suddenly yelled encouragement to a player who was sliding headfirst into third for a stolen base.

The players and spectators recognized Russell at once, and they gathered around him, eager to tell him their likes and dislikes. He listened patiently to everything they had to say. He explained some of the rules and regulations to them and answered their questions about why some of the restrictions were necessary. He laughed with them, and when they began unloading their burdens, he told them about some of his own troubles, principally in getting funds to finance the prison system adequately. Pretty soon he was calling some of the girls by their first names and was talking to them about their home towns.

"Mr. Russell," one of the inmates interrupted, "we'd like some music out here. Couldn't we have a band come play so we could dance?"

"I'll see about it," he promised.

Billie Jean was a player on one of the teams that afternoon, and I introduced her to Director Russell. He knew the story of her taming the bloodhounds, but neither of them mentioned it. I also introduced to him several other prisoners whose acquaintance I had made in police court. They were all eager for news from Montgomery, and I tried to brief them on what I thought would interest them, especially news from the police station.

Our outdoor conference could have gone on indefinitely, but supper time came and the women were summoned into the prison for their evening meal. As they walked across the hard-packed red clay yard, they called back to Russell, "Come to see us again! Please don't forget us! Come back!"

He didn't forget. That very night the band from Draper Prison, inmate musicians all, arrived at Tutwiler Prison, and for the next hour and a half there was music and dancing in the dining hall.

Perhaps it was because he was impressed by my friendship with Billie Jean, or maybe because I seemed to get along well with the other inmates that Russell offered me the job as warden of Tutwiler Prison. I thought he was teasing, but he was not. I declined immediately!

In addition to prison stories, Sharpley liked murder and violence ("They sell papers"), so the death of David Blakey was his kind of story. It was the first big murder story I covered.

The story started simply. On November 17, 1941, I wrote a brief article saying that David T. Blakey, thirty-two, had been missing from his home, 525 South Lawrence Street, for five days. Law enforcement officers were broadcasting his description and asking for help in locating him.

Blakey lived with his mother and was said to be a model son who would do nothing to distress her. Neighbors described him as a friendly fellow who would do a favor for anybody and who often picked up strangers, especially soldiers, and rode them around with him. He was a big man, six feet tall and 185 pounds, with unusually broad shoulders. When he left home the night of November 12 for a dinner engagement, he was wearing a blue double-breasted suit, black oxfords, a dark grey hat, and a dark grey belted overcoat. He was driving a 1941 two-door Ford sedan with Scotch plaid seat covers.

The car was found on a lonely county road near Haleyville, 190 miles from Montgomery, four days later. It had been burned and the license plates removed. Identification of the vehicle was made by the Montgomery dealer from whom Blakey had purchased the car in August. "This looks as if there must have been foul play," Police Chief Ralph King stated. He had no further comments for the press. But he was absolutely right.

Blakey's bloated body was found in the Alabama River by a rural housewife who was out looking for her stray turkeys. Coroner M. B. Kirkpatrick reported that Blakey's arms were bound in front, his jaw broken, and his head battered, and it appeared he had been choked before his body was thrown into the river. I wrote that even the toughest officers paled at the brutality of the crime. I wrote all the gory details, even told about the "gliding, wheeling buzzards" that attracted the housewife to the spot where the half-submerged body was found. I was glad I did not have to see that body.

I did see the murderer, Ellis Howard Rowe, when he was brought to Montgomery from Haleyville on December 2. He was tall and lanky, and his dark hair was tousled. He had on dirty khaki pants and a leather jacket over a dark sweater. He was chewing gum.

Rowe signed a confession in which he implicated a companion, Charlie Ray Holland, in the murder. Holland, nineteen, was arrested soon after Rowe was taken into custody, and he, too, confessed to his part in the crime.

The pair told of meeting Blakey in front of a downtown cafe where he was standing on the sidewalk trimming his fingernails with his pocket knife. They fell into conversation with him about some of the girls inside the cafe. "If we had a car, we could date those girls," Rowe said. Blakey offered the use of his car, and the three of them began a round of honky-tonks, a night of drinking that ended with Blakey being beaten and thrown, still pleading for his life, into the river and Rowe and Holland fleeing in his car.

Holland returned to his home in Montgomery, but Rowe, according to his confession, spent three days riding his girl friends around in Blakey's car before he burned the vehicle, threw the license plates into a water tank, and caught a freight train for Aberdeen, South Dakota, where he had heard his brother was living. (Rowe was later leaving Haleyville than he had planned to be, he told officers. He fell asleep beside the railroad track while waiting for his transportation to arrive, and policemen waked him up and chased him away. He then had to wait for the next freight.)

Failing to find his brother in Aberdeen, Rowe caught a freight train back to Haleyville. He was arrested by Alabama Highway Patrolmen less than five seconds after his feet touched the chert in the railroad yard of that northwest Alabama town.

In their confessions, both Rowe and Holland told of an argument between Rowe and Blakey over who should drive the car. Blakey, who was driving, had sideswiped a passing vehicle, and Rowe demanded to be allowed to drive, the two said. When Blakey protested, saying that he was not drunk, Rowe struck him in the head with a rock. Both Rowe and Holland then beat Blakey about his head and body, tied his hands together and shoved his limp body into the back seat of his car. They then drove to the bridge that spans the Alabama River on U.S. 31 where Blakey was heaved into the murky waters below.

Rowe reportedly told officers, "I don't know whether he was dead then or not. He didn't make any sounds after we hit him in the head."

Holland told a different story. According to his account, Rowe forced Blakey, staggering from the brutal beating he had received, to get out of the car and walk to the center of the bridge. With each step Blakey begged to be allowed to live. As Blakey stood by the bridge rail, imploring his captors to release him, Rowe suddenly stooped, grabbed Blakey's feet and hurled him over the side of the bridge.

"Oh, God—" Blakey screamed as he plummeted into the dark waters of the river, Holland recounted. At that point Holland ended his account of the night of horror.

It was my first murder story, as I said, and Sharpley seemed pleased with it. I got by-lines, of course, with banner headlines and four-column pictures of the two suspects in Highway Patrol custody. The story sold papers, too: Blakey's family was well known in Montgomery.

Justice moved more swiftly then, nearly fifty years ago, than it does today. Rowe was tried before Circuit Judge Eugene Carter on December 15, and Holland's trial was held the following day. Rowe showed little emotion during his trial, sitting almost motionless, until the solicitor began to read his confession aloud. All through that reading, Rowe's slender fingers folded and unfolded an empty match box.

It took the jury only thirty-six minutes to find Rowe guilty of murder in the first degree and to recommend the death penalty. Holland was found by his jury to have been an accomplice in the murder of Blakey.

Judge Carter, on December 19, 1941, sentenced Row to die in the electric chair on January 23, 1942. Holland received a sentence of life in prison. Rowe told the judge, "I'd like to say I was drunk during all the time it happened." His attorney, E. W. Wadsworth, immediately filed a motion to appeal. Holland made no comment when his sentence was read. He reddened but remained silent.

In less than six weeks, David Blakey's murderers had been apprehended, tried and sentenced.

Rowe's appeal was not successful, but on the eve of his execution date, March 24, 1943, Governor Chauncey Sparks commuted his death sentence to life imprisonment. During that clemency hearing, Rowe, wearing white prison garb, wiped away tears as his grandmother and sister pleaded with the governor to spare his life.

It was a letter to Rowe from an older sister, whose whereabouts no member of the family knew, that moved the governor to spare the prisoner's life. The letter was read aloud by Prison Chaplain E. M. Parkman.

I love you. God alone knows why I have stayed away from my brothers and sisters for eleven long years. I guess I expected you and Guy to stay my kid brothers always.

But we kids never really had a home, did we? A shack by the railroad track or in the worst parts of any town we ever lived in. Hardly clothes enough to cover our skins. Maybe we had enough to eat at times; then again we didn't.

I don't guess you remember the time our aunts and uncles had to take up a collection in Nauvoo, Alabama, and send to Illinois to get us back to Nauvoo after Dad had left us stranded, but I do. I also remember the two-room shanty we were living in.

Then we were divided out among our kinfolks. It was you, Guy and Delphia who caught the devil. I guess I got more schooling than the rest of you but I never finished the eighth grade.

Dear, what I am trying to say is that you never had a chance. It's not you that should be on trial for your life. Oh, no. I know you should not have done what you did, but I will never condemn you. . . .

In closing this letter part of my heart goes with it. May God bless you and have mercy on your soul. I love you always.

The letter was enclosed in a box of food which the sister sent to Rowe his first Christmas in prison. There was no return address.

In a part of his statement commuting Rowe's sentence, Governor Sparks said, "I am not willing to inflict the extreme penalty on one who has had such environments in life and such a poor chance to make a man." He also noted that the crime seemed to have sprung from circumstances in which all the parties were involved, and he pointed out that Holland, apparently equally guilty, was given a life sentence.

Rowe, prison records show, died in prison about eighteen months later. Holland was released after serving several years of his term.

I also wrote about several other murders, including the case of Mrs. Andrew Armstrong, who died in bed at her home on Holcombe Street. Mrs. Armstrong's fourteen-year-old daughter, Leila, went next door and told the neighbor that her mother was dead. Neighbors found Mrs. Armstrong lying in bed in a pool of blood. They called the coroner, Dr. B. M. Kirkpatrick, who, after a preliminary examination, said he believed the woman had died as the result of a hemorrhage.

The body was moved to a mortuary. At the mortuary, an employee posed a question: "If this lady died of a hemorrhage, why is there a bullet hole in her head?" The question was an embarrassment to Coroner Kirkpatrick. The woman did indeed have a bullet hole at the base of her brain. Leila was booked on suspicion of murder.

Although Leila was only fourteen, the papers carried a detailed account of her involvement in her mother's death. Juveniles, back then, were not protected from publicity, from having their names and deeds made public. Detective Lieutenants Cobb and Frizzle, who investigated the shooting, said Leila refused to talk to them, but she did talk freely with her father, a railroad engineer, when he came in from an all-night run. He arrived soon after the shooting. Leila told her father that her mother's death was accidental.

According to investigators, Leila had gone about her early morning household duties after the shooting. She prepared food for her baby sister, twelve months old, and she got dressed for school. (She was enrolled at Baldwin Junior High School where she was described as a good eighth-grade student with the second highest possible grade in conduct.) After she had dressed and had put the house in order, Leila went next door to report that her mother was dead. When police arrived at the Armstrong home, Leila volunteered to help them locate the empty cartridge shell. She burst into tears when the shell was found on the floor near a bed.

She was calm and composed shortly after noon when her father accompanied her to police headquarters to be booked on suspicion of murder. Only red circles around her dark eyes gave evidence that she had been weeping. Her father stood with his hand on her shoulder while she answered routine questions asked by Lieut. Joe Seaman. Leila's hands were thrust deep into the pockets of her sky-blue sport coat, and she kept her back turned to her questioner. She spelled her name for the officer in a clear, firm voice, but her answers to other questions were in monosyllables.

"The shooting was an accident, wasn't it?" Chief of Detectives Paul Rapport asked.

"Yes, sir," Leila replied.

"You're sorry it happened, aren't you?" the chief continued.

"Yes, sir." Her back was still turned toward him.

Armstrong told officers that Leila said the gun discharged accidentally when she was taking it down from the wall. Leila and her father did some rifle practice when the family lived out on the edge of town, Armstrong said, and she had her own gun.

The coroner, who by then had done a more thorough investigation, declared "the physical findings and autopsy indicate that it was not an accident." There were powder burns on Mrs. Armstrong's pillow, he said, a detail he had overlooked in his initial investigation.

Leila was transferred to the custody of the juvenile court and charged with delinquency, the customary charge for juvenile law-breaking of any kind. Once the transfer was made, juvenile court authorities declined to discuss the case. Leila was permitted to attend the funeral services for her mother.

The most sensational murder I covered for the *Journal* was what was commonly referred to as "the feather duster murder case."

I was on vacation when Dave A. Holloway, widely known Montgomery insurance salesman and businessman, was found murdered in his Gilmer Avenue home, but I returned in time to cover the trial of his wife, Kathryn Lawrence Holloway, who was charged with the crime.

That trial was held on July 21 and July 22, 1943, only ten days after Holloway's battered, bloody, nude body was found on the sleeping porch of his home. Coroner M. B. Kirkpatrick, who was called to the scene by a neighbor, reported that he found 150 wounds on the body, adding,

"No human being could have taken such a beating and lived." Chief of Detectives Paul Rapport declared that the deceased had received enough blows to "kill two mules."

The murder weapon, which was found behind some books in a closet, was a stick about eighteen inches long and weighing only a few ounces. It appeared to be a feather duster handle. There were dried blood and hairs on one end of that stick.

Mrs. Holloway, some fifteen years her husband's junior, testified for more than an hour in her own defense. Because of the extremely personal and sordid nature of her testimony, the courtroom was cleared of spectators during part of the time she was on the stand. I was permitted to stay and listen.

"Did you kill your husband?" one of her attorneys asked.

"I did not," she replied in a firm, steady voice. She looked directly into the eyes of the twelve men who would decide her fate.

It was an ugly story the red-haired defendant told, yet she told it convincingly and with a touch of dignity. At times she appeared embarrassed and lowered her eyes as she told of the happenings at the Holloway home the night of July 10 and the early morning hours of July 11.

She began her story by telling of meeting her husband in the lobby of the post office the night of July 10. The couple had been married less than a year and were separated at the time. Holloway, she told the jury, asked her to go home with him and spend the night. She accepted his invitation. She told of a night that began with "talking of nothing else other than being happy together," of a quarrel that developed into a fight, and of Holloway's hitting her with a small black stick.

"He threw me on the floor and jabbed me with the stick," she told the jury. The couple tussled over possession of the stick until she finally gained possession of it and hit him several times. The battle for the stick continued, with brief lulls in the action, both upstairs and down, the defendant testified, until Holloway told her to take the car keys and go get her clothes from the Alabama Street abode where she had been staying.

"He was standing in the door between the dressing room and the sleeping porch when I left," she said. That was the last time she saw him alive. She told of getting her belongings from Alabama Street, returning to the Holloway house and going upstairs to bed.

Upon awaking about ten o'clock the next morning, her testimony continued, she went downstairs, where she found Holloway lying in bed on the sleeping porch with blood coming from his nose. She tried to wash the blood away, she recounted, and she begged her husband to speak to her. When he failed to respond, she ran next door, still in her night dress, for help.

Mrs. Holloway, her own testimony finished, sat calmly, scarcely changing expression, in the sultry courtroom as witness after witness told of the condition of the victim's beaten body, of the bloodstains in the rooms on the first floor of the house. She wore an aqua dress, and her red hair was arranged in a long bob. Seated beside her with his arm across the back of her chair was her father, a retired minister from Florida. He and she were the only witnesses called by the defense. The father testified briefly, establishing Mrs. Holloway's age as forty-one. Pre-trial reports of the case had listed her age as thirty-three.

The prosecution, led by veteran solicitor Temp Seibels,

and the defense attorneys, Norman Spann and James S. Parrish, completed their final arguments to the jury on the second day of the trial, in the late afternoon. The jury deliberated one hour and thirty-five minutes.

Mrs. Holloway, supported by her brother-in-law, stood pale and expressionless when the jury returned its verdict: Not guilty. The spectators burst into applause.

I don't know what happened to the short black stick with dried blood and hairs on one end of it.

Although murders of white citizens were usually given big stories in the paper, the murders of Negroes were virtually ignored. "Negress Bound Over on Murder Charge," which rated one paragraph, and "Negro Bound Over in Death of Wife," a two-paragraph story, were fairly typical of the coverage given such crimes.

Not much more attention was paid when Negroes were shot by law enforcement officers. Such shootings were almost always justified as self-defense. They did not occur often, testimony perhaps to an unrecorded understanding—if not acceptance—of the relationship between the races.

Montgomery was a segregated city, as was the entire South, in my newspaper days there. Signs marked the white and colored waiting rooms at the bus stations, train stations, doctors' and dentists' offices. Public drinking fountains were plainly designated "white" and "colored." Public gatherings, even those centered around the war effort, were segregated.

In my account of the November 11, 1941, Armistice Day parade up Dexter Avenue (I called it the most spectacular observance of Armistice Day in Montgomery's history), I wrote, "A group of negro soldiers from Maxwell Field, a negro band, Red Cross and groups from various negro ex-service organizations made up the final section of the parade." The same story announced that a section in the balcony at the City Auditorium had been reserved for any Negroes who wished to hear the patriotic speech to be delivered there at eight o'clock.

That was the way things were.

Chapter 6

MANY ITEMS were in scarce supply by 1943. Lines formed quickly, almost magically, outside stores when word spread that cigarettes, chewing gum, diapers, chocolate bars, Kleenex, hair pins, bobby pins or nylon hose were available. Sometimes the people waiting in line did not even know what was being sold; if it was scarce, they wanted it.

Nylon hose were real treasures. They were saved for wearing on the most special of occasions, and between wearings they were put in a glass jar with a close-fitting top and kept in the refrigerator. This treatment was supposed to prolong the life of the hose. One of the first things I did when I took over Allen Rankin's desk at the *Journal* was to put wide strips of adhesive tape down the wooden legs of the desk and the chair so I would not snag my hose on splinters. The male reporters were amused.

When the weather got warm enough, we women went barelegged. To hide the unattractive whiteness of our legs (there was no time to lie out in the sun and get a tan), we covered them with pancake makeup. The makeup, available in several shades, came in solid flat cakes and was applied with a damp sponge. There were some leg makeups that came in liquid form, but they were rather expensive. But whether solid or liquid, the makeup ran in streaks in Montgomery's summer heat. Paths of sweat left legs looking like maps of the Alabama river systems. It was hard to decide between having legs that were pale as the belly of a dead fish or having strangely patterned skin.

Summers were hot in the *Journal's* news room. There were big fans in the new building but no air conditioning. There was not even any cool drinking water on our floor. For some unknown reason, the fine modern drinking fountain that was supposed to supply cold water had never been hooked up. We complained, but nobody did anything.

Then George Perry took action. George was in charge of the Associated Press's teletype machines, and thus was not an employee of the newspaper. He had a barbed sense of humor and he was a good actor, often appearing in the skits and pageants staged at Sara Crist's apartment.

R. F. Hudson, owner of the two newspapers, was proud of his new building and liked to take business associates on tours of the facility. When George would hear one of the Hudson-conducted tour groups approaching the newsroom, he would come out of the Associated Press office, gasping and panting, and stagger toward the water fountain. Failing to get the fountain to work, George would heave a pitiful sigh and drape himself across the dry machine, as though he had collapsed from thirst. His timing was perfect. Mr. Hudson appeared to ignore George's performances, and we who were employed by that gentleman kept busy at our typewriters, but George captured the attention and stirred the curiosity of the visitors.

After three or four of George's shows, we arrived at work one morning to find the fountain working perfectly. We referred to that cold drinking water as George's Great Gift.

George was a fine story teller. He used to tell us about the adventures he and his brother Bill had when they went to New York to Seek Fame and Fortune. Bill wanted to be a singer, and I've forgotten what George's talent was. Anyhow, it was during the depression, and they almost starved to death. Even dishwashing jobs were scarce. Bill made a little money singing at weddings and funerals every now and then (he would fill his pockets with food to share with George in their garret room), but they had almost no money.

For entertainment, they would take a dime each, money saved for this specific purpose, and go to a picture show. After they had seen the movie, they would begin to fight each other, creating such a disturbance that the usher would ask them to leave. They demanded—and got—a refund. Those two dimes paid for their entertainment for a long time.

On one occasion, Bill was given tickets, ringside seats, to a world championship boxing match at Madison Square Garden. He and George were delighted. They walked the many blocks from their room to the Garden, but they didn't mind; they'd have something to write home about and to remember for a lifetime. But when they got to the Garden, they couldn't get in. They were required to pay tax on their tickets, and they had no money. They sat on the curb and cried.

Came New Year's Eve, an event to which they had looked forward with great eagerness. For years they had read about and heard about the New Year's Eve celebration at Times Square, and now they were going to get to be a part of that vast excitement. And it was free. They couldn't wait!

Just as the brothers were about to leave their room, an acquaintance stopped by with a bottle of cheap wine. "Let's drink a toast to the New Year," he said. So they did, a couple of toasts. The next thing George and Bill knew, the sun was shining in the window of their room. It was January 1, and they had missed New Year's Eve at Times Square completely.

George told me some mighty sad stories.

However, his brother Bill did finally find Fame and Fortune in New York. He became the featured soloist on the Carnation Milk Hour, and music lovers all over the country sat by their radios to hear Bill Perry sing every week.

George, when I knew him, was a patriotic young man who wanted to serve his country in the armed forces, but every time he reported for a physical examination, he fainted. Just the sight of a white-coated doctor or a nurse in her starched uniform made him keel over.

I listened to George tell about how embarrassed he got when he joined a bunch of draftees or volunteers to have his physical. "I faint right there in front of everybody. I can't help it," he said. "I know they think I'm must putting on an act to keep out of the service." Remembering what good acts George could put on, I sort of wondered about his fainting spells myself. Of course, I didn't tell him so.

Well, one night George took me to a movie at the Paramount Theatre. About halfway through, there was a hospital scene with doctors and nurses. I heard a rustling sound beside me, and when I turned to look, I saw George slowly sliding out of his seat and disappearing under the rows of seats in front of us. It took two ushers, several spectators and me to extricate him from an entanglement of legs (human and metallic), stretch him out in the aisle and revive him. "Doctors do that to him," I said by the way of explanation as we left the theater.

George never did get into the army.

Those wartime years in Montgomery it was rare to see a young man in civilian clothes; uniforms were everywhere. War bond drives, scrap metal collections, victory gardens, news of area servicemen, and rationing regulations filled the columns of local news in the paper.

Even the character of police court changed. Cases involving the thefts of tires, sugar and chickens became more common. Tires were precious items, and thieves became expert at snatching them from automobiles. Chief of Police Ralph King urged persons attending night football games, circuses and fairs to lock their tires to the wheels, using chains and padlocks, before leaving their vehicles in parking lots or on the street. "Of course," the police chief said, "we are going to take every precaution to see that tires are not stolen. But tires are one of the most priceless possessions of Montgomerians these days, and we feel that they should be warned of the possible danger."

City Detective Lieutenants Chancellor and Davis, about the same time, announced the arrest of twenty-three-year-old Charlie Thomas, who they speculated was responsible for as many as fifty tire thefts.

Thomas, known in local circles as High John, had a rather unusual method of operation. He, officers said, would steal a tire and then, a few days later, sell it back to his victim. Thomas carried on his scheme successfully for quite some time and might even have become more successful if he had kept a promise to his young nephew.

The nephew, it seems, became disgruntled when High John failed to carry out his promise to take him to the picture show. The angry lad told on his uncle, told a neighbor that the tire he had bought from High John was the very one that had been stolen from his car—by High John. Word reached the police, and they took appropriate action.

When High John's case came before Judge Scott in police court, the defendant was given the longest sentence ever handed out by the judge: three years in the state prison. Thomas pleaded guilty to three charges of stealing tires and was given a year in each case. During his testimony, Thomas said he had left one of the stolen tires on a sidewalk when he discovered it had a hole in it.

Thomas's accomplice in the thefts, Willie Mae Thornton, was given a three-month hard labor sentence despite her plea that she had done nothing but "tote some little old pieces of iron." Those pieces of iron, officers, said, were tools used to remove the tires from the cars.

Rubber was so scarce along about then that children's tire swings, old tires used as borders for flower beds, even tires long ago related to junk piles were reclaimed and sent to salvage centers. As the tread on automobile tires wore thinner and thinner, traffic officers began taking brooms in their patrol cars to sweep away glass and other sharp objects that might injure tires. The *Journal* ran a picture of a traffic sergeant sweeping up glass on Fairview Avenue. The caption said he hoped his wife did not learn of his deftness with a broom.

Drives aimed at collecting scrap metals also continued and were well publicized. Every time I saw a pile of rusting metal waiting to be shipped to a reclamation center, I thought of the times when I, as a little girl, had stood on our front porch with my father and watched trains pass with long strings of cars piled high with scrap iron on its way to Mobile to be shipped to Japan. "The Japs are going to shoot that metal back at us some day," my daddy prophesied.

The need for scrap metal prompted law enforcement officers to increase their zeal in confiscating illegal slot machines. Actually, it may have been a grand jury report and the actions of Mrs. Jett Thomas, resourceful chairman of the Montgomery drive for scrap aluminum, that prompted the action. Mrs. Thomas called on Sheriff Addie Mosley and Police Commissioner W. P. Screws to seize and rend all roscoes in order to salvage the aluminum therein.

"It is time that these iniquitous devices did some good in the world," Mrs. Thomas declared. "They can right some of the wrong they have done by going to a glorious end— supplying material we need so vitally to defend our country! These vicious machines must be scrapped for national defense!" It was a fine, stirring speech.

Sheriff Mosley responded immediately by axing perhaps a dozen of the offensive roscoes (why are the one-armed bandits called that?), and Commissioner Screws directed the police department to stop the operation of all slot machines and other such gambling equipment at once. The sheriff was happy to pose, ax in hand, with a pile of the illegal machines as he prepared to salvage the aluminum from them.

78

Safety devices, known as Walk-O-Lites, peculiar to Montgomery, also fell victim to the wartime metal shortages. These neon lights with their "Walk" and "Wait" messages were installed in metal casings on the sidewalks at busy downtown crossings about 1940. The invention of a Montgomerian, some of these sidewalk traffic lights had worked loose from their moorings and were a hazard to unwary pedestrians. The manufacturers were unable to get the metal needed to repair the Walk-O-Lites, so they asked the city to remove them.

Saffold Joseph, one of Montgomery's downtown characters and a frequent visitor to the *Alabama Journal*'s newsroom, may have been somewhat responsible for the removal of those Walk-O-Lites. Mr. Joseph, a slight, usually silent man of undetermined age, had a room somewhere in the vicinity of the newspaper offices. Every day he patrolled the sidewalks of downtown Montgomery, making sure that they were safe for pedestrians. He carried with him a brown paper sack, a spatula and several pieces of chalk. He used the spatula to scoop up banana peels carelessly discarded on the sidewalks, and he deposited the peels in the paper sacks, keeping careful count of each day's collection. He used the chalk to draw arrows calling attention to broken or cracked sidewalks, loose paving stones and such, any hazard that might cause a pedestrian to trip and fall.

For several weeks before their removal, Mr. Joseph had chalked "Loose Casing" warnings on many of the Walk-O-Lites. His daily public safety work was reduced when the city replaced the wobbly devices with good, substantial concrete, material that would not need his chalked warnings for a long, long time.

Montgomery during the early 1940s had a fleet of red, beat-up taxis known as Dime Taxis that would take passengers anywhere in the city limits for ten cents. The Dime Taxi seldom delivered a passenger to his or her destination immediately, but after awhile patient people got where they wanted to go. The general procedure was for the driver to wait until he had four passengers (sometimes more if lap-sitting was not objected to) going in the same general direction before he began his trip.

I rode in Dime Taxis hundreds of times when I worked in Montgomery. Daytime rides were all right, but circuitous rides with strangers late at night sometimes made me feel a bit uneasy. This was particularly true when I would return from a weekend visit to Birmingham and would arrive at the Union Station around midnight.

One day I laughingly mentioned to Chief Rapport that I felt the need of police protection on those rides out to Cloverdale Park. He surprised me by saying, "You can have it. Just call us."

So I did. Thereafter, when my train arrived at the crowded station (all stations were crowded at all hours those war years), I would call police headquarters, and an unmarked car driven by plainclothes detectives would come pick me up and take me home. It was a splendid arrangement.

Then one night I made my customary call from the station, found a seat on one of the long wooden benches partitioned by armrests, and waited for my ride to come. I was sitting there calmly, watching all the people and wondering where they were from and where they were going, when two uniformed policemen pushed through the heavy double doors and scanned the waiting room.

One of the officers shouted, "There she is! Get her!"

They descended upon me, snatched up my suitcase and hustled me past scores of puzzled and surprised spectators out to the waiting police car. My "arrest" at the train station provided laughs and conversation at police headquarters for days. I let them enjoy their joke—the rides home were worth it.

Even Sharpley was not above playing a small joke on me.

In October, 1941, he sent me to the bus station to write about three busloads of draftees being sent to the induction station at Anniston. I wrote a sentimental story about sweethearts holding back tears, and the absence of military bands, and the strange silence on the buses, and the newsboy hawking papers with glaring headlines telling of bitter fighting on the Russian front, and strangers who stared thoughtfully at the young men before stepping out of the station into the sunlight, and baggage boys whistling off-key, and the draftees who leaned out of windows to wave as the buses left the station, and the draftees who never looked back.

It was the kind of coverage I felt sure Sharpley would like. He gave it a four-column headline on page one, and he even brought me one of the first papers off the press. His bringing me a paper was a rare and unexpected courtesy.

Then I saw my story. Under my by-line Sharpley had written a new lead. "This morning I helped kiss the boys goodbye," it said. I couldn't believe it!

Sharpley was delighted. He reveled in the teasing I received: "Did you kiss all seventy-six of the boys?" "Surprised you needed help with that assignment!" And other such remarks.

Chapter 7

LOOKING back after almost half a century, I am struck by how many of the "odd eggs" I remember from my first newspaper job, by the variety of people I met. There were not only the law enforcement officers, the politicians, the criminals, the artists (art takes many forms), but there were also people such as Dr. Luther L. Hill whom I interviewed on the eve of his eightieth birthday. The doctor, spry and alert, leaned back in his chair at his roll-top desk and talked about performing the first successful operation for suture of the heart in America, back in 1902.

"It was strange how that thing happened just at the right time, almost as if it were planned," Dr. Hill recalled. "I had read everything I could find about operations on the heart which two surgeons performed in Europe. I even wrote to one of the surgeons to ask questions, and I had studied until I knew every step of the procedure. Then one day one of my colleagues rushed into my office and shouted that a little Negro boy had suffered a heart wound in a fight in a cemetery over near where Cramton Bowl is now. I gathered up my instruments and went with him. In that Negro house I performed the first successful heart operation in America."

He chuckled as he added that recently a big Negro man walked into his office, introduced himself and said, "Doctor, I's the boy you sewed up that heart fuh. I just want you to know it don't give me no trouble."

Dr. Hill talked of the homes where he performed his early operations, comparing them with modern (1942) operating rooms in hospitals. "The first abdominal operation I ever saw I did in a rented room on the first block of South Court Street," he recalled.

Most such home surgery was done on the kitchen table, but if the table was too short, Dr. Hill used to take a door off its hinges, place it on two sturdy pieces of furniture, cover it with a sheet and proceed with the operation. "We doctors did the best we could, used whatever facilities were available back then."

When he was only twenty-one years old, the farm-reared Dr. Hill spent six months in London studying surgery under the renowned Lord Joseph Lister. It was for the teacher that he named his son, Lister Hill. That son chose politics rather than medicine as his profession. During his years as a member of the U.S. Senate, he sponsored legislation aimed at improving health care and hospital facilities, especially in rural areas. Senator Hill never forgot all those tales he heard his father tell.

Two big game hunters, Osa Johnson and Frank ("Bring-Em-Back-Alive") Buck, brought their tales of adventure to Montgomery. The war had changed the plans of each of them, and they had substituted lecture tours for tracking exotic animals and birds in their native habitats.

No one in the hotel lobby where she held a press conference recognized Osa Johnson. If she had come swaying into the hotel atop an elephant with a high-powered rifle and a movie camera under one arm and pet tiger under the other, there would have been cries, of, "Look! There's Osa Johnson!" and she would have been besieged with requests for autographs. But no one associated the small woman with the pug nose, the big brown eyes and the frivolous hat with the famous adventuress who had photographed wild animals and primitive people all over the world.

Her fourth book, *I Married Adventure,* had recently been published. The foreword, written by the president of the American Museum of Natural History, said in part, "When Osa married Martin, she married his destiny too. Home was to be a schooner in the South Seas, a raft in Borneo, a tent on safari, a hut in the black Congo, sometimes a dash of Paris, interludes of an apartment on Fifth Avenue—but always a place to be going from.

This is a tale of two lives, a boy and a girl from Kansas, pushing their horizons into far places."

She talked about the years when she and her husband, Martin Johnson, had explored remote islands and photographed native tribesmen who had never before seen white faces, and she talked about returning to Alabama to go fishing with Governor Frank Dixon. Somehow I felt that fishing in an Alabama pond would be unappealingly dull to a woman who had dined with head-hunters in Borneo and been chased by cannibals in the New Hebrides.

Frank Buck was easier to recognize, even though he wore

a soft felt hat instead of a pith helmet and a conservative pin-striped business suit instead of the khaki shorts and open shirt he was usually photographed wearing. He conducted his interview while he breakfasted on honeydew melon, toast with orange marmalade, and coffee, a breakfast that seemed somehow out of character.

While he munched on his melon, he talked about growing up in Texas where he kept so many rattlesnakes, birds, and flying squirrels in his father's barn that the farm animals had to be moved to other quarters.

As was Osa Johnson, he was touring the country on a lecture circuit while he waited for the war to end. He was eager to resume his career of capturing wild animals for zoos and circuses, he said. If Governor Dixon invited him on a fishing trip, Buck did not mention it.

Lord and Lady Halifax came to Montgomery in the spring of 1943 to thank the residents "who have given our British boys such a pleasant stay in this country." The British ambassador and his wife were met at Union Station (the train arrived earlier than scheduled) by a welcoming committee that included Governor Chauncey Sparks, Mayor Cyrus Brown, and military officers.

At a press conference at the governor's mansion, Lord Halifax slumped comfortably in a big chair, all six feet six inches of him. "I believe we could talk easier if our chairs were pulled closer together," he said to the reporters, and he moved his chair forward. He settled himself again and had begun an informal conversation when an aide tip-toed in and whispered a message in his ear. Lord Halifax laughed and moved his chair again. In his original move he had placed one of the chair's legs firmly on the buzzer used to summon servants from the kitchen.

The British visitor had other difficulties getting the press conference underway. In the group of reporters was a woman who had hosted a morning radio show for long, long time, a show with a title, as I recall, something like "Around The Town." She considered herself a true radio personality and as such she made her presence known at all gatherings.

She and her husband had at one time either lived in England or made prolonged visits there, and she had many friends, all of noble rank, about whom she wished recent news. "How are my good friends, Lord and Lady So and So?" she asked the ambassador, and before he could finish answering, she was inquiring about a particular duke and duchess, also her good friends, followed by requests for news of Lord and Lady Such and Such.

The ambassador was very patient, more patient than the newspaper reporters (none of us knew anybody in England personally) who were eager to hear what Lord Halifax had to say about the progress of the war. Just as he was beginning to answer a reporter's question, the woman leaned forward and interrupted again.

"Oh, please tell me about my dear, dear friends Lord and Lady Nonesuch. It has been ten years since I've seen them."

"Then let me assure you," Lord Halifax replied icily, "that they are ten years older." The press conference proceeded normally from that point on.

Frank M. Dixon was governor when I went to work for the *Journal,* and after I had been on the staff for a few months, Sharpley decreed that I should attend Governor Dixon's afternoon press conferences.

His meetings with the press were relaxed and informal, with a lot of laughter mixed in with the news-gathering. Most afternoons Fred Taylor, political reporter for the *Birmingham News,* Tommy Maynor of the Associated Press, Forrest Castleberry of the United Press, and I met with the governor. Out-of-town newsmen frequently attended the conferences, but the four of us "regulars" were there nearly every day.

Governor Dixon was a wartime governor (1939–1943), and I think he used his news conferences as periods of relaxation. He had no adversarial or confrontational relationship with the press, but he was always a good—and reliable—source of news.

The press corps sometimes put on skits, political satires of sorts, for the governor's entertainment. Our skit-writing was done at Sara Crist's upstairs apartment in her mother's big house on Cloverdale Road when we gathered, as we often did, for Saturday night parties there. We considered our productions quite clever (the one I remember best was a political take-off on Dickens's *A Christmas Carol*), and so did the governor.

Most afternoons one of the state prisoners from Kilby who worked as trusties at the Capitol would bring in a tray of coffee or Coca-Colas for our refreshment. As those drinks became more difficult to get, scarcer in the years of rationing, tall glasses of water were substituted. The governor kept bowls of peanuts and pecans, prison grown, on his desk.

Forrest Castleberry, a bachelor, had an apartment near the Capitol, and one of the Capitol trusties used to go clean it up during his lunch hour every day. One afternoon during our press conference, the trusty came into the governor's office and said, "'Cuse me, Mr. Forrest, but I found this by yo' bed when I was cleaning up today. I couldn't find but one of them." He handed Forrest an earring, holding it up so everybody could see it.

"Sho' is pretty, ain't it?" the trusty said. Forrest didn't say anything. Governor Dixon never stopped teasing Forrest about that earring.

One afternoon our press conference was interrupted by a commotion outside the governor's office, out in the wide marble halls of the Capitol. We hurried out to see what was happening, and we saw two young ladies, clerks in the Department of Revenue, riding bicycles up and down the corridor.

They were trying out the new bicycles ordered by the state purchasing agent for state employees to ride to work. The wartime shortage of automobile tires had prompted many state employees to seek alternate methods of transportation. One hundred and twenty-five bicycles were ordered for their use, but only forty-seven were delivered, and there was little hope that any more would be available.

"Think you can pedal up Goat Hill?" one onlooker asked. The Capitol sits atop the steepest hill in Montgomery, and those heavy, balloon-tired bicycles had no gears: it was all pedal power.

"We may be too tired to work when we get up here—but it will be fun coasting home!" one of the cyclists replied.

"At least I won't be expected to ride a bicycle!" Governor Dixon told the press. He had been a pilot in World War I and lost a leg when he was shot down over Germany.

Governor Dixon genuinely liked most people and was politically smart enough to act as if he liked them even if he didn't. However, he literally despised Eleanor Roosevelt and was outspoken about his feelings.

At our final press conference, just before he was to turn over his office to Governor Chauncey Sparks (January, 1943), we reporters entertained the outgoing governor by reading an epic poem highlighting the events of his administration. Then we presented him with a big box, elegantly wrapped. Inside was a large, framed picture of Eleanor Roosevelt on which was inscribed, "To my dear friend, Frank Dixon, with love always, Eleanor."

Governor Dixon laughed until he was gasping for breath. Then he threatened to beat us all with the heavy picture frame if we didn't get out of his office immediately. We left. Laughing.

While Dixon was governor, former Governor Bibb Graves died. Graves had served two terms as governor, 1927–31 and 1935–39. I covered his funeral services that March day in 1942. The sanctuary at the First Christian Church in Montgomery was filled with friends and admirers an hour before the funeral service began, and more than 1500 people stood outside. In that crowd outside the church was Governor Frank Dixon. I do not know why space for him had not been reserved inside the building.

I had not known Governor Graves (his term had ended before I went to work for the *Journal*), had met him only once. That meeting came while I was a student at Huntingdon College. My friend, Frances Lanier, and I went to the Capitol one day in search of material for our column, "The Newshounds," in the college paper. We chanced to meet with some "real" reporters who invited us to attend Governor Graves's press conference with them. We did.

At one point, the governor asked if there were any questions. I had not planned to ask a question, but I did. "Governor," I heard myself saying, "I have heard that all great men sleep with one foot out from under the cover. Do you?"

Governor Graves was almost as surprised at being asked the question as I was at asking it. After all these years, I have forgotten exactly what his reply was, but it dealt with being cold-natured, wanting to keep his feet warm, and thus failing to meet this criterion for greatness. He also admitted to pulling the cover off his wife on very cold nights.

I watched the inauguration of Governor Chauncey Sparks on a rainy January day in 1943. The showers, which had doused the dignitaries—and the spectators—during the early part of the parade, stopped just before the actual inaugural ceremonies began.

Chauncey Sparks was able to remove his raincoat and appear in his inaugural outfit of striped pants, cutaway coat, stiff shirt and wide cravat. "I never had on striped pants before in my life," he told friends before the ceremony. "They aren't often worn in Barbour County! This outfit cost me more than it cost me to get elected!" So he was glad he could show his expensive finery off.

Maybe it was his excitement over being so finely dressed that was to blame, but somehow Governor Sparks miscounted the cannons' roar of his twenty-one-gun salute: he made three false starts on his inaugural address only to be drowned out each time by the thunder of the guns.

For the first time in history, the car that brought the

outgoing and incoming governors up Dexter Avenue was driven by a woman, an attractive blonde named Edna Thompson, instead of by a uniformed male chauffeur. Governor Sparks was a bachelor, which may have had an influence on the choice of chauffeur.

The new governor was friendly with the press, but he never established the relaxed relationship Governor Dixon fostered. The Capitol reporters never wrote poems or put on skits for him nor did he ever receive a gag gift from them. His style was a bit more reserved. I left Montgomery a few months after he became governor, so I never had close ties with his administration, don't have many personal memories of Governor Sparks.

I do recall that in the fall of 1945, when I was on the staff of the *Birmingham News,* I went down to Washington County in southwest Alabama to the Bull Pen Hunting Club where Governor Sparks was the guest of honor. He killed two turkeys, both gobblers, with one shot. The legal limit was one gobbler per day, but since the double killing was an accident, no arrests were made. That night after supper, sitting in the shadow of the fire and listening to hunters tell tales, Governor Sparks held my hand. He held it a long time, as though he did not know how to let go, and I wasn't quite sure either.

One other bit of Governor Sparks trivia: he neglected to register for a liquor ration book when that commodity was placed on the list of rationed items in August, 1943. Said he forgot. Registration for a liquor ration book had to be done in person. Some folks said the governor did not want to be seen standing in line at the registration site, said he might lose the support of some Prohibitionist friends.

Each coupon in the liquor ration book entitled the holder to purchase a pint of spirits a week. It was possible to purchase a quart of whiskey by surrendering two ration stamps—but no more could be bought for the next two weeks. The system created real hardships for some people, but apparently not for the governor.

There was talk of an earlier conflict, memories of long-ago battles, when eight veterans of the War Between the States gathered in Montgomery for the forty-first annual reunion of the Alabama Division United Confederate Veterans in May, 1941. Colonel J. W. Moore of Selma was the youngest veteran present; he was only ninety years old.

This tottering remnant of the once strong Confederate forces met to share recollections of Shiloh and Chickamauga, of Sherman and of Lee. And if some of those recollections were tangled in the fringes of their minds, it really did not matter. There was no need to talk of the unforgettable bond that held them together, their love for their native South.

Sitting on the edge of the group of veterans were three Negro body servants who had gone with their white masters to fight the war. Simon Phillips was the most talkative of the trio. He could not hear well, but he could talk endlessly about his master, Bride Watkins of Hale County, and how they chased "that scoundrel Sherman" from Chattanooga to Gadsden and how "me and Mr. Bride and them other soldiers was so hungry we et anything we could chew." Simon told everybody he talked to, "Them Yankees didn't whip us, they overpowered us!" and he gleefully put into his pockets the nickels and dimes his listeners gave him.

Dr. R. A. Gwynn of Birmingham, a retired Baptist evangelist, didn't talk much, though he was the best preserved of the trio. "I don't remember good," he said. "I don't even know how old I am."

Richard Watson, the last surviving slave in Montgomery, made only one remark during the convention. He broke a long silence to say, "I's the last man in Montgomery who fought in the war. Looks like they would make me a general soon."

President Roosevelt addressed the nation by radio while that Confederate reunion was in session. At the Jefferson Davis Hotel, headquarters for the convention, the old men cupped their hands behind their ears and leaned forward on their canes toward the radio. And though they could not hear everything he said, they voiced approval of their president's speech, pledged their full support to the government they had tried to defeat a long lifetime ago. That 1941 gathering may have been the last Confederate reunion held in Alabama.

I told Louise Pickens about that Confederate reunion, just as I told her about "the feather duster murder" and Billie Jean's escape and Forrest Castleberry's missing earring and other important happenings in Montgomery.

Louise was blind. She and her boxer, Rama, operated a concession stand on the corner across from the *Advertiser-Journal* building. Louise knew nearly everybody in Montgomery and she kept up with nearly everything that went on. An attractive brunette with a happy, outgoing personality, she did not look or act as if she were blind, and sometimes even her close friends would forget that she could not see.

One afternoon I had stopped by her stand for a Coca-Cola and a visit when a traveling photographer, the kind who shows samples of the almost-lifelike likenesses his company produces, walked in, bought some cigarettes, chatted a bit and then began his sales spiel. He pulled a portrait out of his batch of samples, thrust it toward her and said, "Look. Isn't that beautiful?"

"I can't see," Louise said.

"Of course you can see! Just look at this quality. Don't you want your family to have a fine picture of you, one like this?" the salesman persisted.

Louise said again, "I can't see." Again the salesman ignored her remarks and continued to implore her to look at the photograph.

"I can't look—I'm blind," Louise responded.

"Blind!" the salesman repeated, still not believing her. "Blind! I've heard hundreds of excuses and brush-offs, but you're the first person who ever claimed to be blind—"

"But she is blind," I interrupted. "She really is blind."

Louise laughed and eased the fellow's embarrassment by saying, "It's all right—don't try to apologize. I think it's a compliment when people don't realize I'm blind."

Louise was a part of our newspaper crowd, came to our parties and went on our outings. She was invited not because anybody felt sorry for her but because she was fun. One Saturday night a crowd of us were going out to eat and dance at a place, probably the Green Lantern, on the outskirts of Montgomery, and we had arranged for Louise to go with a young second lieutenant from Maxwell, someone she had never met. His name was Barney.

"Don't tell Barney that Louise is blind. I'll bet you five

dollars he'll never know it unless she tells him," I said to Barney's friend who was providing transportation for part of the crowd. He agreed to the wager.

You could tell that Barney was delighted with Louise the moment he saw her, and they were surely the best-looking couple on the dance floor. Louise was a marvelous dancer. She could also swim, ride horseback and bowl, although she did not demonstrate those talents that night, of course.

When the evening ended and Barney walked Louise to the door of her apartment, she said to him, "Thank you, Barney, for a great evening. And now you can tell all your friends you had a real blind date. I'm blind." Barney was stunned. Not too stunned though to ask her for a date the next Saturday night.

My five-dollar bet was easy money.

Louise was one of the friends I hated to leave when I moved from Montgomery. We had fancied up her name by then. Once after she complained about the plainness of "just Louise," I began calling her Louisa Melissa Petunia Begonia, and the names stuck. There were other names in that long string, more fancy flower names, but I've forgotten them now.

I did leave Montgomery in the late summer of 1943, moved to Birmingham to work for the U.S. Treasury Department promoting the sales of war bonds in Alabama. For more than a year I had handled the publicity for war bonds in the *Alabama Journal,* and my stories caught the attention of officials in the state office. They offered me a job. It paid so much more than I was making at the *Journal* that I did not hesitate a decent period of time before accepting.

But I did hate to leave Montgomery. I love that town.

My year with the Treasury Department does not properly belong in this book, since I was not working for a newspaper then. I left my title of Odd-Egg Editor back in Montgomery.

However, I did have experiences in my new job which influenced my newspaper career later. To begin with, I had to have a car. New cars were not available then (1943) and even dependable used cars were hard to find. After inquiring around a bit, I was directed to a reputable dealer who sold me a well-used Studebaker Champion for $300. I borrowed the money from my doctor brother to pay for it. My car had no air conditioning, of course, nor did it have power anything, but it did have overdrive which was supposed to be a great advance in automotive engineering.

That car took me all over Alabama, into towns where I'd never been before: Buhl, Lisman, Hackleburg, Ohatchee, Flomaton, Tunnel Springs and others. I met every newspaper editor in the state and every radio station manager.

My war bond job provided me with my one claim to fame: I have spent the night in every one of Alabama's sixty-seven counties. I knew people in all of those counties, too, probate judges, mayors, lawyers, garden club presidents, bankers, people active in civic affairs.

"If you want to get things done in a town, county or state, you have to know who the leaders are so you can motivate them to work with you," Marc Ray Clement, Administrator of the Alabama War Savings Staff, told me. "You identify those leaders and you keep in personal touch with them and you let them know how important each one of them is to the success of the project. Never let them forget. Never."

Marc Ray (everybody called him "Foots") was the finest organizer and the best politician I've ever known. He never ran for public office himself (he was a lawyer in Tuscaloosa, graduate of the University of Alabama), but he knew how to manage political campaigns. He knew how to manage war bond campaigns, too. Alabama was the only state in the union in which every county met every quota in every war bond drive.

Foots was a big man. His tall frame carried weight of more than 250 pounds, so he needed his large feet. They *were* large. He talked on the telephone almost constantly, rocking slowly back and forth in his desk chair as he talked. With that telephone he kept in touch with the network of county war bond chairmen, congratulating them, prodding them, offering suggestions, taking whatever tone the situation needed. Those chairmen and their co-workers were volunteers, proud and successful volunteers, and Foots meant to keep them that way.

I spent a lot of time traveling. I helped to arrange war bond rallies, to publicize them, to get speakers and bands for the events all over the state. Our most effective speakers were wounded servicemen who volunteered for such assignments. They were given leave from hospitals, where they were recovering from their wounds, to give personal accounts of the atrocities they had witnessed and had themselves suffered. No patriotic American could keep from investing in war bonds ("Back the Attack!") after hearing one of those speeches.

The only problem was that since the servicemen volunteered for this duty, and since they were free from military supervision, they sometimes failed to appear at the appointed place and time. It did not happen often, but it did happen. The fellows had been in combat areas, been deprived of feminine companionship for so long that they were easily diverted by pretty girls. On one occasion when my wounded serviceman failed to appear at a rally, I found that he had decided to get married instead of making a talk. Fortunately I was able to find a substitute speaker.

My writing during this period was mostly the fill-in-the-blanks kind: "County War Bond Chairman _____ announced today that _____ County has recorded sales of _____ for the month." Then would follow several paragraphs quoting said chairman about the importance of investing in freedom.

I completely ignored the training Sharpley had given me about posing people for photographs. I squeezed as many people as the viewfinder would accommodate into every picture. "People like to see their names and their pictures in the paper," Foots told me. "Makes them happy." With the help of cooperative newspaper editors, I made lots of people happy.

The trouble was, I wasn't real happy. I liked traveling around the state and meeting new people, but I missed working for a newspaper. So when Vincent Townsend, city editor of the *Birmingham News,* offered me a job, I took it.

I learned a lot while I worked for the Treasury Department, learned a lot about my native state and about dealing with people. I also learned to take a seventy-five-watt light bulb with me when I traveled: light bulbs in most hotel rooms were too dim to read by at night.

Above: My first press pass
entitled me to attend
movies free and write
movie reviews for my
hometown newspaper.
Left: A young, naive
Kathryn Tucker, soon
after I became Odd-Egg
Editor at the *Alabama
Journal*

Right: I get a lesson in bayonet combat from an expert at an Alabama National Guard camp. My major concern was that my precious stockings might get torn!
Below: Explorer Osa Johnson talks to me about her exciting adventures in some of the world's most remote places, far from the lobby of the Jeff Davis Hotel in Montgomery where the interview was held.

Above: A 1942 Christmas party at Sara Crist's apartment had Santa Claus plus an assortment of newspaper folk, friends, and other guests. Louise Pickens is seated in the center of the group, and George Perry is to her right. Judge John Scott is wearing convict stripes. *Left:* Judge Scott gets dressed for his role in a skit. His costume is authentic, straight from the Montgomery city jail.

Above: Lord Halifax, seated center, meets the press at the Alabama governor's mansion. From left are Forrest Castleberry, United Press; Fred Taylor, *Birmingham News;* Colonel George Joerg, Maxwell Field; Kathryn Tucker, *Alabama Journal;* Lord Halifax; two radio people; and Tommy Maynor, Associated Press.

Governor Frank Dixon, right, discusses a political issue with, from left, Forrest Castleberry, United Press; Fred Taylor, *Birmingham News;* Tommy Maynor, Associated Press; and me. I appear to be taking notes, but I am really writing the final scene of a political satire.

Deer and wild turkey were plentiful at the Bull Pen Hunting Club, but *Life* photographer Bill Shrout, *below,* and I did not fire a single shot.

Above: This press pass, dated March 9, 1965, gave me access to the area in and around the Dallas County Courthouse where Sheriff Jim Clark and his deputies patrolled. *Below:* Sheriff Clark questions a young demonstrator outside the Dallas County Courthouse on a February day in 1965.

Above: Black citizens waiting to register to vote
gather outside the Dallas
County Courthouse in the
spring of 1965. *Left:* Stokely
Carmichael and I, both
amused by some now-
forgotten joke, emerge
from the Federal Building
in Selma where I had been
covering federal court.

I show off a photographic award presented to me at the 1969 Alabama Associated Press meeting. I also got awards for a feature story and for spot news coverage that year.

Chapter 8

THE *Birmingham News* was the biggest newspaper in the state, much bigger than the *Alabama Journal*. There were more people on the *News*'s copy desk than were in the whole newsroom back in Montgomery. I was not given a descriptive title at the *News*, but my early duties involved traveling around the state in search of feature articles.

One of my assignments was to go down to Choctaw County and do a story about Alabama's first oil field. I was to take my own pictures, Vincent informed me. I had to inform him that I did not know how to use a Graflex camera. Jack House, a *News* reporter who knew how to do almost everything, gave me a quick lesson in the operation of the bulky camera and wished me luck. I filled the camera case with loaded film holders and flash bulbs (those things burned painfully if they went off in your hand) and headed for Choctaw County. All the way there I kept reviewing what Jack had told me about lens openings and shutter speeds and especially about remembering to turn the film holder over before I took a second picture. This was before the day of film packs.

I knew several people in the county through my work on the War Savings staff, and they introduced me to the oil drillers on the well site close to Gilbertown. At that well site I learned a whole new language with words such as "roughnecks," "wildcatters," and "ratholes" scattered in it, and I prayed that I was doing all the things Jack House had told me to do with the camera.

The Hunt Oil Company had brought in its first well about a mile and a half west of Gilbertown, on February 16, 1944. It was named the Avon R. Jackson Well Number One, and it produced sixty barrels of oil per day, mighty low by Texas standards. Even that small flow of oil created excitement (it was Alabama's first producing oil well), and by the time A. R. Jackson Number Two came in on February 29, there wasn't a place to stay in Gilbertown nor was there land or oil leases for sale. The town was packed with oil men and speculators.

As I recall, I spent two nights in a small second-floor room over a bus station or drug store in downtown Butler, the county seat, about twenty miles north of Gilbertown. I spent a full day at the oil field (a third well had been brought in by then) looking, listening and taking pictures.

The distance from Birmingham to Gilbertown was a little less than 200 miles, but it was a long, roundabout drive. There were no interstates or even four-lane highways, so it was at best a 4 1/2-hour drive. My drive back to Birmingham seemed to take forever. I had taken a dozen photographs (film and flash bulbs were scarce, and every shot had to count). I had horrible thoughts, obsessive fears, of having double-exposed at least half of my pictures and of coming up with blanks on the other half. It was indeed a long drive home.

The pictures turned out fine; not a single double-exposure or a single blank. Vincent ran a half page of my photographs with my story. And my by-line. I was off to a good start.

My salary was considerably better at the *News* than it had been on the *Journal*. (Male reporters on the *News* were probably paid more than women were—I'm not sure about that—but at least by the time I joined the *News*'s staff women were accepted in that once-male world and were judged by their competence, not by their sex.) I was paid $100 for my first week, the most money I had ever had for a week's work in my life. I didn't get that much weekly pay again though; I had claimed overtime (quite justifiably) on my first time sheet, and before I filled out another one, I learned that overtime was not claimed except in the most unusual circumstances.

Vincent Townsend was a remarkable city editor. He moved to Birmingham from Port Tampa, Florida, when he was in grammar school (1911), graduated from Birmingham-Southern College, and lived in Birmingham the rest of his life. He had reliable news sources throughout the area, and he always knew what was going on. He not only knew what was happening, he knew why it was happening, knew the background of every local story. And he expected his reporters to accumulate that same store of knowledge. "Keep asking, 'Why?'" he used to say. "Get it right. Get it right."

He could spot a sloppy job of reporting before he had

read the first paragraph of a story. He never screamed or threw tantrums the way city editors in the movies did, but his voice was icy when he asked, "Is this the best you can do?" So were his eyes.

Away from work, Vincent was relaxed, knew how to have a good time. At Gus Gulas's restaurant, around the corner on Fifth Avenue, he told stories while he ate pie (always sprinkled generously with salt) and drank cup after cup of coffee. He knew stores about nearly everybody in Birmingham. He was at his best telling newspaper stories, and one of his favorites was about a young reporter who had covered the city hall beat for the *News*.

There were several versions of the story, but the way Vincent told it the reporter got bored at the city hall one Saturday night (nothing newsworthy ever happened on Saturday nights), so he left and went to a movie. It was a good movie, and he was sorry when it ended, sorry that he had to go back around to the city hall. He hadn't eaten anything except popcorn and two candy bars for nearly three hours, so he thought he would stop on the way back to his beat and get a bite to eat. But first, he figured, he'd better check in with the city desk, just to reassure them that he was on the job in case anything happened.

He stopped at a pay phone in the theatre lobby to make his call. "Just wanted you to know things are quiet at the city hall, and—"

"Quiet, hell!" the city editor stormed. "The city hall is burning down! Every fire unit and every reporter in town is there—except you! Where are you?" The ex-reporter hung up and started looking for a job that very night, Vincent said.

So when Vincent assigned me to cover the courthouse and said to "look out for fires," I knew what he meant, even though my beat was not the city hall.

Although I had covered civil and criminal trials, I had never handled a courthouse beat on a routine basis. I knew about city government and state government, having been assigned to both, but the functions of the county were new to me. Not only did I have to learn the workings of the county court system, I had to familiarize myself with the duties of the probate judge, the county commission, tax collector, tax assessor, treasurer, and other county offices. Furthermore, I needed to know personally the men (they were all men) who held those positions.

Oddly enough, my best teacher was the reporter from our rival paper, the *Birmingham Post*. I'll call him Percy.

Percy was a veteran courthouse reporter, had been covering the place so long he knew every office holder and every secretary, knew their families, knew everything about them. Percy could get straight to the source of any news story and have all the facts assembled before most reporters got their pencils sharpened. He was amazing.

Percy could have gone far in the newspaper profession if he had not had an unfortunate weakness. Percy, as they say, was "bad to drink." He would sometimes go for weeks and weeks without taking a drink, but then the urge would hit him, and he'd go on a binge. He had many friends in the courthouse, and when he was not able to function properly, they would cover up for him, telephone information on breaking news stories to his office. Sometimes the friends would even write whole stories under Percy's by-line and send them over to the *Post* by a janitor. Nobody wanted Percy to lose his job.

Came a day when Percy felt he had to have a drink, but he had no money. His friends would do nearly anything for him, but they would not lend him money. Percy was desperate. He went down into a basement storage room at the courthouse and got an armload of new brooms. Then he put on dark glasses, sat on the front steps of the courthouse and pretended to be a blind broom salesman. Percy did right well with his new enterprise. He would sell a broom, go buy a bottle of beer, and then return to his stand. He'd sell another broom, buy another bottle of beer. Sales were good because his price was cheap. Percy was mighty pleased with the success of his scheme. Then a deputy sheriff happened to walk by. The deputy recognized the "blind" peddler immediately, confiscated his remaining wares and hustled him off toward jail.

Once again friends came to Percy's aid. They rescued him from the clutches of the law and reimbursed the county for the brooms Percy had sold. They even called his office with some valid-sounding excuse about why he had not been able to write any stories that morning.

Among Percy's courthouse friends was a young, devout, idealistic secretary who believed that Percy would stop drinking if he would read and study the Bible daily. When she talked to Percy about this method of reform, she was shocked to learn that he did not own a Bible. She was a young woman of action as well as of faith, so she immediately started a fund to buy a Bible for Percy. She put a glass jar on her desk with a sign that said PERCY'S BIBLE FUND, and whenever her co-workers had spare change, they'd drop it into the jar. Not many co-workers shared her faith, but they were willing to cooperate with any project that might save Percy from the snares of strong drink.

The secretary was pleased with the growth of the fund: she wanted to buy Percy a really nice Bible, a red-letter edition with illustrations and good print and with his name embossed in gold on the cover. Every time Percy came into her office, she showed him how rapidly the jar was filling up. "Won't be long before we'll have enough in your Bible fund to buy your Bible," she would promise him. Percy would smile and nod and mutter something about how deeply touched he was by her concern for his welfare. He was sincere about it, too.

Well, one morning I walked into the press room at the courthouse and Percy was sitting at his desk sobbing out loud. He was quite drunk. "What in the world is the matter, Percy?" I asked. I'd seen him drunk, but I had never seen him cry before.

"I've done an awful thing, an awful thing," he said, looking at me with teary, bleary eyes. "I've drunk up the Bible fund!"

There was another reporter in Birmingham, this one on the staff of the *News,* who was occasionally cursed by close association with Demon Rum. His name was Charley, and he looked like a blond cherub, though he surely did not behave like one.

One morning there was a serious shortage of yellow copy pencils in the newsroom. Even the short nubs of pencils were missing. So was Charley. Searchers finally found Charley crawling along a flower bed on the side of the Birmingham Public Library. He would step every few feet, dig a hole and bury a pencil in it.

"Charley, what are you doing?" a fellow reporter asked.

"I'm planting pencils so they'll grow into typewriters. Come help me," Charley replied.

They swear he really believed he could raise a crop of typewriters right beside the library.

We courthouse reporters had a press room for our use, and each of us had a desk, a chair and a telephone there. The only other piece of furniture was a long couch. The place was not fancy but it was adequate. My routine was to go by the major offices looking for news as soon as I arrived each morning and then go to the press room to write my stories and telephone them to the newspaper.

One morning when I tried to enter the press room, I found the door locked from the inside, and I heard whisperings, a man's voice and a woman's voice, in the room. I knocked discretely and identified myself.

"Come back later," the man's voice said. I went down the hall to borrow the use of a telephone so I could call in my story.

For several mornings I found the door locked, heard voices (I knew who the man's voice belonged to—he was on the staff of the *News*) and had to find somewhere else to communicate with my office. I was irked. And curious.

I did some careful inquiring and learned that the man, who had a wife and a houseful of children, was meeting his lady love in the press room early every morning. She, I learned, was a wrestler. I didn't know exactly how to handle the situation, but I knew something had to be done to put a stop to or at least change the location of the couple's early morning trysts.

My situation became desperate when Vincent said to me,

"Miss Tucker, I have tried to reach you at the press room several times, and nobody answers the telephone. Remember the city hall fire?" Talk about dilemmas! I did not want to lose my job nor did I want to tattle on an errant husband or confront a lady wrestler.

What I did was to persuade a janitor to adjust the latch on the press room's door so that it could not be locked from the inside. He was glad to put the lock out of commission permanently in exchange for a package of cigarettes.

My solution worked perfectly. Deprived of their guarantee of privacy, the couple found another meeting place, and I was right there in the press room to answer the telephone when Vincent called.

As punishment for one of his periods of drunkenness (his friends could not always protect him), the *Post*'s city editor moved Percy from his courthouse beat and put him tó work on the copy desk. Percy hated it. To take Percy's place as courthouse reporter, the *Post* hired a beautiful young blonde, one of the best-looking females I ever saw. Her features, her figure, her clothes, her carriage—everything about her was perfect. And she knew it.

The male officeholders were smitten by this new reporter, just couldn't do enough to help her gather news. They tried to outdo each other to make sure that Miss Post, as they called her, knew everything that was happening in the courthouse and knew it first. It appeared that hard times were ahead for me—I could not compete with that siren.

My salvation came from an unexpected but welcome source. Though their bosses fawned over Miss Post, the

secretaries hated her. Maybe they were envious of her per-
fection or maybe she did high-hat them, as they accused her
of doing. I don't know. All I know is that those secretaries
formed a network to make sure that Miss Post did not
scoop me. They passed along to me news tips that their
bosses didn't even know about until they read the story in
the *News*.

It was during this Miss Post period that one of the secretaries called to tell me that I might find an interesting story
at the county jail if I hurried. I hurried. The officers were
booking a woman on a murder charge. The woman, past
middle age, was saying to the officers, "I'm glad it's finally
over with, glad to turn myself in."

The woman had turned herself in to the sheriff and had
confessed to him that she had killed her husband more than
ten years earlier. The murder was in the unsolved file, but
she had never been a suspect, had never been questioned.
She was alone, and she seemed uncertain as to what she was
expected to do.

"Would you like for me to walk to your cell with you?" I
asked. She seemed grateful for my offer. "Do you need
anything? Toothpaste or a comb?"

She shook her head.

I don't know who she thought I was, a jail matron or a
social worker or what. Since I did not have a pencil and pad
with me, I'm sure she never thought I was a reporter.

Slowly at first and then in a torrent of words, she began
to tell me of the agony of living with guilt. "It's been like
walking along the top of a high board fence. Balancing and
putting one foot in front of the other real carefully but

knowing all the time that one day you're going to fall. For ten years I've been waiting to fall, dreading it but knowing it was coming. I couldn't stand it any longer. Waiting. Trying to keep my balance. For ten years I've been afraid to talk, afraid I'd give my secret away. Do you know what it's like to live with a fear and a dread like that?"

I got a five-dollar bonus for the story I wrote about that woman. It was the only bonus I ever got at the *News*. But my conscience hurt me.

It must have been the fall of 1944, the first fall I worked for the *News*, that Vincent sent me down to the Wiregrass section of Alabama to do a story on the peanut harvest. Peanuts were that area's biggest money crop, and they also contributed to the war effort by providing food and oil. They needed harvesting. Manpower was critically short, and the peanuts would have rotted in the fields had not the War Department sent some 3,000 prisoners of war to help gather the crop.

Most of the prisoners were Germans, few of them spoke any English, and almost none of them had ever seen peanuts growing before. However, with the help of an interpreter and with demonstrations in the fields, they learned quickly how to loosen the soil around the plants, pull up the vines and stack them to dry. They were surprised to see that the peanuts grew underground like small tubers.

Vincent assigned me to get a story and pictures of the former Nazi soldiers working in the fields. The fall weather was beautiful, and I welcomed a drive down to southeast Alabama.

The local military authorities had approved the story and

photographs, and I was assigned a military policeman, a captain, to take me to a field where a crew of prisoners was working. The captain parked his army vehicle on the shoulder of the country road, and he parted the strands of barbed wire so I could crawl through the fence that sur-rounded the field. As he handed me my Graflex camera, he said, "Take all the pictures you want to. I'll be right here when you're ready to leave."

I walked across the field, stepping over rows of peanuts, to get near some prisoners who were stacking the vines to dry. I made all my camera adjustments, checked the shutter speed and lens opening, and moved around to get the per-fect composition for the pictures I wanted. As I raised my camera to my eye, I saw a scary sight: one of the prisoners was running toward me with a pitchfork! He was screaming something in German.

I turned and ran toward the car, leaping across peanut rows as I ran. My big camera was something of a hindrance, but I dared not drop it. My would-be assailant would have destroyed it with one jab of his pitchfork.

As my camera and I neared the safety of the fence, I looked back and saw that the prisoner had stopped chasing me. He stood about thirty feet away, brandishing his pitch-fork in a menacing manner and hurling German invectives at me. I expected some show of protection from my mili-tary escort, but all he did was lift up the wire so I could get back through. "Don't believe that German wanted to have his picture made," he commented.

I'm not sure whether or not I had violated any rules of the Geneva Convention in attempting to photograph pris-oners of war without their signed permissions. Maybe that's what my chaser was yelling about. If that was the problem, my next effort at violating the Convention's rules was more successful. We (my MP was still driving) found another group of prisoners who were cooperative and even smiled for the camera. Even so, I made sure I had an unobstructed path to the car before I began clicking the shutter!

During my time at the *News*, the central focus of the paper was on reporting the progress of the war. Banner headlines told of battles in the European, North African and Pacific theatres, and smaller stories dealt with rationing, war bond sales, production quotas, and news of Alabama servicemen and -women.

Many women had volunteered for services. My college friend and co-author of "The Newshounds," Frances Lanier, as unmilitary a person as could be imagined, was a lieutenant in the Marines. She demonstrated her lack of martial skills one bright California day when she marched a platoon of Marine recruits into a brick wall—with a general looking on! She literally never learned her left hand from her right.

This unfortunate episode was never reported in the *News*, but the paper did carry long columns daily of news of Alabamians in uniform. Those columns of personal items were the most read, clipped and saved of any feature in the paper.

Cornelia Lively and Barbara Parks edited and wrote the news of service personnel, getting their material from the stacks of releases sent in by public relations offices around the world. Their typewriters were seldom silent; they turned out far more copy than anybody else on the paper.

Some newsroom wag termed their by-line a description of an ideal date: Lively and Parks. Both Cornelia and Barbara were war wives. Cornelia's husband, Bob, was a lieutenant commander in the navy, and Barbara's husband, Guyton, was an army major.

Barbara Parks and I shared an apartment with Nell Megginson over the mountain in English Village. The apartment (2854 Fairway Drive) was sub-leased to us by Nell's boss at IBM when he was called into military service, and he leased it completely furnished.

We were fortunate. Desirable housing was difficult to find, almost non-existent, in Birmingham those war years. That industrial town was jammed with thousands of workers and their families. The steel mills, the furnaces, the plants were working around the clock to produce war goods. It was not unusual for three workers, each assigned to a different shift, to share a room at a rooming house, taking turns sleeping in the one bed.

We were blessed not only with pleasant quarters but also with a clean environment. Smog hung heavy in downtown Birmingham most days, and a film of grime covered every unprotected surface. Fresh white collars and cuffs were dingy before noon. Those early ring-around-the-collar detergent ads must have been conceived in Birmingham.

Our apartment had only one disadvantage: it was very near Vincent Townsend's house. Many mornings I would be awakened by the telephone and Vincent's gravelly voice saying, "Miss Tucker, I'm saving gasoline. Please come pick me up on your way to work. I'm ready now."

I'd put on my clothes on the way to the door and comb my hair going down the sidewalk. Vincent did not like to be kept waiting, and he despised tardiness. I did my best to keep him happy. Actually, I enjoyed those early morning (we were at work by seven o'clock) rides with Vincent. He told me stories about Birmingham people and he talked about the future of the Magic City, about its potential as a great medical center. Occasionally on clear mornings when we had crested the mountain and had begun our descent into the heart of the city, Vincent would say, "Now slow down. Look at Birmingham spread out there below you. It's beautiful, isn't it?"

Vincent loved Birmingham. He saw beauty beneath its cloak of industrial pollution, and he loved it even during the racial turmoil of the 1960s, those years when he tried to bring reason and calm to a city scarred by hatred and violence.

A few times Vincent waked me at night to go out and cover a story. One morning about two o'clock he called and said, "Are you awake, Miss Tucker? The president of the World Bank is out at the airport waiting for a flight. Go interview him." All the way to the airport I wondered what I would ask the man. I knew nothing about finances, certainly not on a world scale, and I wasn't at all sure what the World Bank was. There was nobody to give me either guidance or background information.

In an airport peopled with sleepy soldiers and bedraggled civilians, it was easy to recognize the man I had come to interview. He was well dressed, alert and distinguished looking, obviously a person of importance. He appeared surprised that a woman had come out long past midnight to interview him. He waited politely for my first question.

I could not think of one sensible thing to ask, so I confessed my ignorance, my utter and complete ignorance, of finances, both world and local. For nearly an hour that learned man talked to me about money and the role it plays in world affairs. He made the concept of a world bank easier to understand than compound interest.

One of my middle-of-the-night airport interviews was with a team of soil conservation experts from South Africa. They were easier for me to talk to. They, too, were surprised that a woman came out to interview them so late at night, and they were even more surprised that I knew about kudzu and lespedeza.

In addition to my late-night interviews and my courthouse beat, Vincent broadened my horizons, as he explained to me, by letting me cover real estate and aviation news. Delta Airlines was just getting started then, and somewhere among my keepsakes I have a tiny sterling silver airline pin, a gift from Delta.

After Marguerite Johnston (her perpetual cheerfulness prompted one *News* switchboard operator to say, "If she steps off that elevator one more morning smiling and greeting everybody so joyously, I'm going to strangle her with this telephone cord!") was sent to Washington as the *News's* Capitol correspondent in 1945, I took over some of her former duties.

One of those duties was to write a weekly column called "Ration Diary," a roundup of news from the Office of Price Administration (OPA) and a reminder of which ration stamps were valid for the coming weeks. "Keep it interesting," Vincent told me. So I mixed in human interest tales such as the one about the woman in a war-crowded Alabama town who called the OPA to ask if she could rent her easy chair for fifteen dollars a month. That's what one of her roomers was paying to sleep in it, she said.

And there was also the announcement that OPA had placed a ceiling price on Hawaiian hula girls. Photographers, the OPA said, had been charging servicemen high prices to have their photographs made with hula girls. Under the new regulations, the servicemen had to pay only a quarter for each girl in the picture with them.

The "Ration Diary," the spring and early summer of 1945, carried the news that feather pillows had fallen in price ("Feathers Fall," the lead-in said); that motorists fortunate enough to qualify for new tires, an almost impossible feat, could purchase synthetic four-ply passenger car tires for $15.20; that the Army was releasing 13,000,000 square feet of outdated panchromatic film for use by civilian photographers, at prices fixed by the OPA; that electric irons, vacuum cleaners, alarm clocks and cameras, all expected to return to the market soon, would cost approximately what similar models cost in 1942.

A June "Ration Diary" began by saying, "Rumors to the effect that Jefferson County citizens who fail to have their blood tests will be denied canning sugar or future ration books are entirely false. The blood testing program and the rationing program are in no way connected, and it would be impossible for the OPA to deny rationed commodities to persons who fail to abide by the state law and have their blood tests made. So help stop those false rumors."

The blood tests referred to in the column were mandatory tests for venereal disease. In a dramatic effort to rid

Alabama of gonorrhea and syphilis, both of which were increasing at alarming rates, the state legislature enacted a law requiring all residents between the ages of fourteen and fifty to have a blood test made. Persons failing to comply with the law were subject to fines of up to $100.

The *Birmingham News* gave its full support to the project, and Vincent named me Venereal Disease Editor. Somehow I never felt entirely comfortable with the title.

The first blood-testing stations opened in Birmingham and Jefferson County in mid-May, 1945, and I, being VD Editor, and also falling in the required age limits, was one of the first persons to be tested. More than 5,000 tests were given the opening day. Testing stations were set up in neighborhood churches, schools, lodge halls and community centers, and the *News* ran a list of the stations and their hours of operation each week. The public was assured that the results of the tests were absolutely confidential.

Early stories about the testing disclosed that the weapon to be used in defeating venereal diseases was a new and magic drug called penicillin. The drug, the stories said, could cure gonorrhea in a few hours and syphilis in nine days. Supplies of penicillin were made available by the government for use in Alabama, marking one of its first widespread uses in treating civilians.

Each person tested was issued a card certifying that the holder had submitted blood for a blood test as required by Act 529, General Acts of Alabama 1943. The cards were numbered and bore the signature of the holder and of the state health officer, Dr. B. F. Austin. Information regarding the color (not race—color), sex, age, weight, and height of the holder was recorded on each card. Testing for white and

Negro citizens was done at separate locations and those locations were so designated in the news stories.

The key to the success of the program was the availability of penicillin for use in treatment of the diseases. The end of hostilities in Europe made the release of the drug possible.

News of the Nazi surrender on May 7, 1945, sparked no boisterous celebration in Birmingham. Confetti and streamers of ticker tape were tossed from windows of tall downtown buildings, but there were no demonstrations of excitement.

"You could tell by looking at their faces which people had loved ones still fighting in the Pacific Theater," the *News*'s coverage of the defeat of the Nazis said. Workers on the production lines in most of Birmingham's defense plants did not learn of the surrender until their lunch break. Employees in the offices heard the news but withheld it so that work would not be interrupted. The state liquor stores were closed, and all retail sales of liquor and beer were suspended. Churches throughout the city were open for prayer.

Vincent, as was his custom, sent reporters out to cover all angles of the story, and then he combined their separate stories into one. I remember going into half a dozen churches to observe the variety of people who came to offer thanks and to pray for the speedy surrender of Japan. The mood was not as somber as it had been on D-Day (June 6, 1944), a day when thousands of residents filed quietly into churches for periods of prayer and meditation, but there was a feeling that exuberance would be premature. The war was only half won. The real celebration would have to wait.

To contrast Birmingham's reaction to the 1945 defeat of the Axis powers with the city's response to the surrender of Germany in 1918, the *News* ran an account of the 1918 celebration with pictures of the occasion.

"By sunup Birmingham was mad, completely mad," the 1918 story said. "Crowds thronged the downtown streets." At three o'clock that afternoon 25,000 people joined in an impromptu parade while 100,000 spectators shouted and yelled. Dignitaries watched from a reviewing stand on the Tutwiler Hotel balcony. Highlight of that mad, mad day was a funeral for the Kaiser. His "corpse" was tied to the back bumper of an ambulance which careened merrily through the streets while the crowds cheered.

Cornelia Lively and Barbara Parks's column, "With Alabama's Fighting Forces," carried long casualty lists on May 8, 1945, the official Victory in Europe Day. The end of hostilities in Europe brought a renewed effort to force the surrender of Japan, and, as always, the *News* used its editorial and news columns to bolster that effort.

I was still promoting the sales of war bonds. When I joined the *News* staff, Vincent listed war bond publicity as one of my assignments. "Can't waste your knowledge in that department," he told me. "But I don't want any fill-in-the-blanks stuff. I want good local coverage." So I continued throughout the war to write war bond promotions, though only those dealing with Jefferson County and Birmingham.

One of the biggest of those promotions came in June, 1945, when two survivors of the team that raised the flag on Iwo Jima brought that famous banner to Birmingham.

"A frayed, faded flag, a flag as famous and with as proud a history as any banner in the world, fluttered from the top of the pole in Woodrow Wilson Park today," my coverage of the event read. "It was the Iwo Jima flag, the symbol the six-man combat team planted atop Mt. Suribachi. That Iwo Jima flag was placed on the park's flagpole by two of the men who, in the thick of Jap snipers and mortar fire, helped hoist it into position atop the volcano on a small Pacific Island." Then I wrote of photographer Joe Rosenthal who snapped the picture that became the most famous photograph of the war.

Marine Pfc. Gene Gagmon and Pharmacist's Mate 2-C John H. Bradley, pictured in Rosenthal's photograph, told the gathering in Woodrow Wilson Park that summer day, "The fellows overseas don't understand why we have to do the fighting and the dying and then have to come back home and beg people to buy war bonds. It seems to us that after we have suffered and bled on some little islands nobody ever heard of, the people safe at home would gladly invest their dollars in our support. We just don't understand why people have to be begged to buy bonds."

Maybe they were shamed by the words of the Iwo Jima heroes or maybe their patriotism was stirred by the sight of the historic flag, but something prodded Jefferson County residents to meet and exceed their Seventh War Loan quota.

Soon after the successful conclusion of the Seventh War Loan drive, I took a vacation and went to New York. I wanted to talk to magazine editors about articles I planned to write, and I wanted to meet people at *Time* for whom I had been answering queries about news in the Birmingham area. I also wanted to see some plays.

Time made reservations for me at The New Weston

Hotel (hotel rooms were still difficult to find in New York) and gave me two tickets to *Oklahoma!* I took my high school sweetheart's mother, who happened to be visiting in New York at the time, to see that stage play. Tickets to *Oklahoma!* were even scarcer than hotel rooms. Our seats were right up front.

Donald Bermingham, one of *Time*'s editors, took me to lunch and gave me a tour of the magazine's offices. We made arrangements for me to write a monthly roundup of newsworthy events in the Birmingham area (it was called a "monthly mailer") and for me to continue to answer their queries.

Over at *Liberty Magazine* (no longer published), I interested William Rae, article editor, in buying an account of Alabama's war on venereal disease.

One night during my visit, longtime friends Eloise and Henry Clay Gipson took me to Billy Rose's night club for dinner (I still called it supper). I'm sure we had an elegant meal, but I was so busy watching for celebrities that I don't recall what I ate.

Except for the lunch with Don Bermingham and the meal at Billy Rose's, my New York dining was done at the Automat and at small, unpretentious and cheap cafeterias. It was in one of those cafeterias that I had my first yogurt. "You won't like it," the server behind the counter warned me. But I did. To me it looked and tasted like clabber. I had grown up on clabber.

That week I saw five Broadway shows, including *Harvey* with Frank Faye in the leading role, saw a movie at Rockefeller Center, rode the subway, strolled in Central Park, read in the New York Public Library and watched the crowds in Times Square.

When time came for me to leave, I was almost flat broke. I had enough money to pay my hotel bill, and I already had my train ticket to Birmingham, but I had little else. After I paid my taxi fare to Grand Central Station and tipped the driver, I had a lone quarter in my purse. That final two-bits went to the red cap who helped me with my bag. He glared in disgust at my stinginess.

The train was crowded with servicemen, as all trains and buses were then, and I thought I was going to have to stand, but a quintet of infantrymen who had turned two seats together offered to let me join them. they were southern boys, as their manners indicated, on their way home to North Carolina.

As the train moved through the night, we slept fitfully, leaning on each other's shoulders, rousing at scheduled stops along the way to watch as passengers got off and others came abroad to take their places. At one of those stops Red Cross volunteers hurried through the coach handing out sandwiches to the men in uniform. When my companions left the train, I ate the half of a sandwich one of them had left behind. It was stale but sustaining, and it was the only food I had on that long ride back to Birmingham.

Chapter 9

BIRMINGHAM's Terminal Station, that elaborate, domed Beaux Arts building on 26th Street, looked more beautiful to me than any of the structures I had seen in New York. A taxi driver took me out to English Village where the manager of the filling station where I traded cashed a check for me. I was affluent enough to pay for my taxi ride home.

After I had eaten whatever food was in our apartment, I took a quick bath, put on fresh clothes and went to the newspaper office to see what had happened during my absence. I also wanted to get my paycheck.

I was greeted by a line of pickets, members of the International Typographical Union, who were on strike. The *Birmingham News* was closed, completely closed.

I knew several of the men walking the picket line, and they slowed their walk to inquire about my New York vacation. "Thought we'd give you a surprise for your homecoming," one of them laughed. Even though the reporters were not union members, I felt somewhat uncomfortable crossing that picket line.

In the newsroom I found most of the staff sitting around reading or listening to a radio. The strike, I learned, had begun on July 12, and could go on indefinitely.

The *Birmingham Age-Herald,* morning paper of the *Birmingham News* company, published a four-page paper on July 12, 1945. The front page was typewritten, and the headlines were hand-lettered.

On the front page was a lengthy statement on the position of the papers regarding the strike. Management's statement called the strike unwarranted, pointed to the tradition of friendly relations between labor and management, and termed union demands for wage increases and changes in working conditions unrealistic and unjustifiable. The statement was signed by James E. Mills, editor, and John W. Frierson, business manager, of the *Birmingham Post* and by J. E. Chappell, president and general manager, Clarence B. Hanson, Jr., publisher, and Harry B. Bradley, business manager, of the *Birmingham News* company. The printers' strike had brought about a truce between the two rival newspaper companies.

A postscript to the statement informed the public that the management of the *Birmingham News* and the *Birmingham Age-Herald* did not intend to attempt to issue its editions regularly during the period of the strike.

For five weeks Birmingham was without a local daily newspaper. During those weeks, we reporters were chagrined to learn that nearly all of the calls about the strike were complaints from people who missed the comic strips. Few readers, it appeared, missed the news or the editorials or even the ads. They did miss the comics.

Vincent did not believe in idleness. It galled him to have his reporters hanging around for eight hours a day doing nothing, yet it also seemed foolishly wasteful to have his reporters gather news when that news could not be printed. He concocted an ingenious plan to keep us busy. Each member of the staff was assigned a section of Birmingham or its environs and told to gather and write a comprehensive history of the area. Vincent dispatched his history gatherers to East Lake, Pratt City, Fairfield, Homewood, Irondale, Central Park and other points.

I was sent to Woodlawn, a pleasant community where, so far as I ever learned, nothing exciting had ever happened. I went by the office each morning, hoping the strike had been settled, and then with pencils and notebook I drove out First Avenue North to Woodlawn. It was not far, a drive of fifteen or twenty minutes. Woodlawn's business district was not impressive, but its side streets bordered with big trees offered welcome shade for parking. July was hot, very hot, in Birmingham.

By working zealously for a few days, I gathered together more information about Woodlawn than anybody would ever need—or want—to know. I knew all about the churches: when they were organized, when the buildings were constructed, how much they cost, who the preachers had been since the very beginning, what the present membership was, even who the various Sunday School classes were named for. I delved into the histories of the schools with the same fervor, and I sought out a dozen older residents who talked with me about days long past. Some of the street names provided a paragraph or so of interest.

When I decided I had done enough research for the day, I

returned to my Studebaker Champion, which I had begun to call my mobile office, and read or worked on my venereal disease article for *Liberty* until time to report back to Vincent.

I was beginning to feel very much at home in Woodlawn as my stay entered its third week. More and more of the residents learned of my mission, and they sought me out to tell me stories of early Woodlawn or to show me old photographs of the area or to suggest the names of people I should talk with. So I did gather a sizable batch of historical information about the neighborhood, though I do not know what became of it. And the editors at *Liberty* bought my article, "Alabama Wars on VD," and paid me $400 for it.

That $400 was the most money I'd ever had at one time in my entire life. I used part of it to buy a desk for Mother to use in her office. Mother was proud of that desk, liked to show it off and tell her friends that it was "a gift from Kathryn—she sold an article to a national magazine." She was always a bit vague and evasive when asked what the article was about.

The strike stretched into August, and the *News* missed printing accounts of an event destined to change the history of the world: the dropping of the atom bomb on Hiroshima.

I remember being in the newsroom, not having gone out to Woodlawn that August 6, and reading the bulletins as they came over the AP teletype, and I recall Vincent's angry frustration about being unable to print the story. Most clearly of all I remember Leroy Sims, AP bureau chief in

Birmingham, perched on the edge of a desk there in the newsroom, chewing on his cigar and explaining to a circle of listeners what the atom bomb was, how it was developed, and the destructive force it carried. I understood very little of what Leroy talked about.

I don't believe that Leroy, talking in his slow drawl against a background of clicking teletypes and clanging bells, each bell announcing a news bulletin about the bombing, understood fully the scope of that bomb's devastation or its effect on the world's future. Nobody did. Even after Leroy had finished his lesson on atomic energy, staff members continued to cluster around the AP room, drawn there by a wonder and a curiosity almost as powerful as the bomb itself.

Among those who came and stood watching the bulletins was Judge Charles N. Feidelson, erudite, articulate, proper columnist for the *News*. He, as always, was immaculately groomed. His pince-nez enhanced his scholarly appearance. He was silent as he read the lines of type clacking from the machine. I noticed, though, that he stopped his reading, clipped his glasses more firmly in place and watched Cornelia Lively as she switched down the hall. "Very disturbing," I heard him mutter. "Very disturbing." I don't think he was commenting on the atom bomb.

And there was gentle Edgar Valentine Smith, his thin shoulders rounded from years of leaning over the copy desk, whose short stories appeared in *Scribner's* and *Harper's* magazines and won for him the O. Henry Memorial Award back before I was old enough to start to school.

And Hugh Sparrow with his sharp facial features and his sharp mind, who covered the Capitol for the *News* and was respected—and feared—by every politician in the state. "I'd rather have J. Edgar Hoover and the whole FBI after me than to have Hugh Sparrow on my trail," state office holders used to say. They meant it. In a time before State Ethics Commissions began to censor unethical behavior, Hugh Sparrow already knew the difference between right and wrong, and he tolerated no deviation from absolute honesty.

Hugh had a frightening ability to sense wrongdoing, and he had the tenacity to ferret out evil at its source, no matter how long his search took or where it led. As is often the case with such dedicated individuals, Hugh lacked a sense of humor. He was also extremely sensitive, perhaps because he was aware that his reporting was not likely to make friends for him, and he was inclined to be impatient.

On the days when he was in Montgomery, it was Hugh's habit to call the *News* at a specific hour each morning and dictate his story over the telephone. Nobody liked to take Hugh's dictation. He spoke in rapid spurts, and he never allowed time for the struggling typist to write such terms as "the Legislature Sub-Committee on Inter-agency Cooperation" or "the Alabama Agricultural Department's Commission on Boll Weevil Eradication." His stories were filled with such terms. He never seemed to realize that they were easier said than written.

If the typist asked him to repeat a sentence or phrase, he took it as a personal affront. "What's the matter? Don't I talk plainly enough? Why can't you understand me?" So every morning as the time neared for Hugh's call from Montgomery, the newsroom began to clear out. It seemed that everybody had to go to the bathroom at the same time.

One morning I let the hour slip up on me. Busy with a story of my own, I was startled to hear Vincent call, "Miss Tucker! Please take Mr. Sparrow's dictation." I turned to Lane Carter whose desk was next to mine. "Lane," I said, "I'll give you fifty cents if you'll take Hugh's dictation."

Lane laughed and picked up his telephone. "What are you laughing about?" Hugh demanded. "What's so funny?" Lane told him, "Kathryn's paying me fifty cents to take your dictation." Hugh slammed down his telephone, and I don't know that he ever called back that day. I do know that he didn't speak to me for weeks.

And there was Lily Mae Caldwell, friend and confidant of movie stars and entertainment celebrities, who conducted the Miss Alabama Pageant each year and who chaperoned the winner to the Atlantic City extravaganza. "You'll recognize Lily Mae," someone told me when I first joined the staff at the *News*. "She's the one who always looks as if she just came in from working in her victory garden."

And Alyce Billings Walker, women's editor, who filled her columns with news of parties, engagements, weddings, and christenings, and who also promoted a hundred Worthy Causes that touched the lives of women.

One night, quite late, Alyce told me the story of Evalena, the cook in the boarding house where Alyce grew up. Evalena sort of "saw after" Alyce, reminded her of her manners, and was prouder than anybody when Alyce won a scholarship to Judson College.

As Alyce's graduation approached, Evalena was troubled because Alyce had nobody to attend the event. She began to save her money so she could go to Judson and be Alyce's family. She put a sugar bowl marked "Alyce's Graduation" on the dining room table, and boarders dropped their spare change in it. By graduation day, Evalena had enough money for her train ticket to Marion and for a new dress to wear. She had to ride in the "colored" train coach (this was in the 1930s), but Alyce and the president of the college were right there at the depot waiting to meet her.

Then there were John Padgett and Hubert Harper, cartoonists, whose sketches and caricatures still hang on walls all across Alabama, and Robert Adams, a photographer with the rare talent of sensing precisely when to press the shutter.

Robert was badly, almost fatally, burned as a child when his Santa Claus suit caught fire during a school pageant. The accident left lasting and disfiguring scars. When war casualties were first being sent to Northington Hospital in Tuscaloosa, Robert was assigned to do a picture story there. In one of those chance meetings that would seem more a creation of fiction than fact, plastic surgeons at Northington met Robert, learned his case history, and volunteered to do bone and skin grafts on the young photographer.

Using new techniques, many of them perfected by treating hundreds of burned servicemen, the surgeon and his friends performed a series of operations on Robert to reshape his facial contours and to increase the mobility of his fingers. Those doctors worked miracles in changing Robert's appearance, but he had two features that needed no change: his shock of red hair and his laughing eyes. They were already just right.

There must have been many other staff members wandering in and out of the newsroom that day, the day the atom bomb was dropped on Hiroshima, but those are the ones I remember most clearly. And clearest of all is the memory of Leroy Simms trying to help us understand the awesome power of the weapon man now possessed. Leroy repeated his discussions on August 9 when an atom bomb fell on Nagasaki. Again Vincent fumed because he had no newspaper in which to print the story.

The strike ended on August 14, the same day that Japan accepted the Allied surrender terms. Members of the printers' union voted that night to return to work, and the next day a four-page combined edition of the *Birmingham News* and the *Birmingham Age-Herald* appeared with the announcement: WAR ENDS.

The first post-strike issue of the *Birmingham News* was published on August 16, and on the front page Cornelia Lively and I shared a by-line on a story telling of Birmingham's celebration of the end of the war. "A Birmingham that hadn't yelled in almost four years, that hadn't snake-danced in twenty-seven, that hadn't showered the streets with tons of paper in a quarter of a century, still remembered how to go wild Tuesday night as it celebrated the greatest day of this generation—the end of the war," we wrote.

We told of staid gentlemen and flower-hatted ladies tooting tin horns and blowing whistles and shouting at passersby and throwing confetti. We wrote of servicemen ambling down the streets kissing, or attempting to kiss, any pretty girls who caught their fancy. We quoted a young brunette who laughed, "I never kissed so many strange men in my life!"

One little boy, we reported, held tight to his mother's

hand and kept asking, "Will Daddy come home now? Will Daddy come home now?"

Some of the downtown churches were open, and worshippers came by twos and threes for moments of prayer and meditation. "And outside the churches the noise grew in volume until it enveloped the city and rolled on to lose itself in the surrounding mountains. Birmingham celebrated Tuesday night. And next morning it woke up, shook the confetti out of its hair and wondered if it were really true, if peace had finally come at last," our story ended.

Vincent ran a full page of pictures with the story: a mother and child kneeling in church, a little boy blowing a paper horn, a soldier kissing a pretty girl, two sailors peeping through the drawn blinds of a locked liquor store, servicemen trying on civilian clothes in a men's shop, a mob scene on 20th Street, a line of young women waving American flags and laughing.

The inside pages of that August 16 *Birmingham News* carried a review of Birmingham and Alabama events since July 11, together with lists of all the births that had occurred and all the marriage licenses that had been issued. On the back page, under the heading of "Catching up with Comics," was a synopsis of what had happened in the lives of comic strip characters during the strike. Readers of "Joe Palooka," "Little Annie Rooney," "Mary Worth," "Tillie," "Snuffy Smith," "The Phantom," "Chief Wahoo and Steve Roper," "Kerry Drake," "Toots and Casper," and "Popeye" were finally happy again.

The war was over. And so was the strike. Things were supposed to settle back to normal, but nobody seemed to remember what normal was.

My "Ration Diary" that August 16 dealt with the joy of being able to drive into a filling station and say, "Fill 'er up!" and of watching the gas gauge swing all the way over to FULL. The OPA announced the end of rationing immediately following President Truman's announcement that hostilities in the Pacific Theatre had ended. Gasoline purchases were back to normal.

The column warned housewives to hang onto their ration books, however, since meats, fats and oils, butter, sugar, shoes, and tires would remain on the ration list until military cutbacks and increased production brought the supply of these items more nearly in balance with demands.

With the return of an adequate supply of gasoline, Vincent began to send his reporters out of Birmingham to cover stories. Although some reporters, depending on their assignments, did get extra gasoline rations during the war, we were always conscious of trying to conserve fuel. To save gas, we often covered out-of-town stories by telephone.

Since it would be impossible to cover a governor's hunting trip by telephone, Vincent sent me down to southwest Alabama "to watch Governor Sparks shoot a deer." I never knew why I was chosen for the assignment, but I went.

Rain had fallen without ceasing for two days and two nights, and by the time I got to the community of Sunflower (in Washington County) the narrow strip of blacktop I was driving on was the only road a sensible motorist would attempt to follow. I stopped at a small store in Sunflower to ask directions to the Bull Pen Hunting Club, scene of the governor's hunt.

"Bull Pen?" the store owner repeated. "That's a place for

men. Sure you want to go there? Never heard of any ladies going to Bull Pen."

I assured her that Bull Pen was where I wanted to go, and she rather hesitantly supplied directions. "You turn left at this corner and you go about six miles down in the swamp. But if you don't know the way, you'll never find it—there're lots of logging roads back in there. And even if you knew the way, you couldn't get there—the roads are impassable."

With those words of encouragement, I turned off the "hard road," as we used to call it, and began slipping and sliding down a red clay passageway toward nothingness. About half an hour and two miles later, I came to another little store where I stopped to inquire if I were heading in the general direction of the hunting club. It was dark inside the store (the door and the wooden shutters at the windows were closed), and I tripped over a Negro man taking a nap on a pile of feed sacks. It turned out that he knew the way to Bull Pen. "Been there lots of times," he told me. I persuaded him to become my guide and chauffeur.

The rain stopped by then, but the log trails, rutted by heavy trucks hauling gum logs out of the swamps, stretched before us like long, watery ribbons. We got stuck. Our situation appeared hopeless until a big, beautiful log truck came along and pulled us out. Half a mile further on, we got stuck again, down past the running board. And the fan belt broke. This time nothing, no log truck, nothing came to our rescue. "We can walk," my companion said. "Ain't but 'bout three miles." So we walked.

Fortunately I had a pair of lace-up hunting boots in the back of the Studebaker. I put those on, and with my handyman carrying my heavy camera and me carrying an armload of flash bulbs, we slipped and slid and waded our way through the swamps toward the Bull Pen Hunting club.

It was an elegant lodge, complete with hot and cold running water, perched on the edge of the Tombigbee River. My spirits rose.

"Lord, miss," the cook greeted me, "them folks ain't coming back here till dark." If he wondered how and why I had found my way to the lodge, he did not say so. "I done sent their dinner to them down in the woods," he continued.

I thought we were already as far "down in the woods" as it was possible to go, but I was wrong. I scraped some of the mud off my boots, drank a cup of coffee, and warmed by the open fire as I formulated a plan of action.

Someone whose identity I never learned had left a Model A Ford, complete with keys, parked at the lodge. I commandeered it. Three sloughs and eight mudholes later, I arrived at the sub-camp, surely one of the most remote spots in the entire state. The hunters were just coming out of the woods as I drove up, and they were obviously shocked to see me—a woman—there. No female had ever before encroached on this male preserve. However, though not without misgivings, they accepted my presence, disheveled, mud-spattered, weary, ill-tempered female that I was.

The governor was there, more genial than usual, as were several other dignitaries, all of them quite willing to have their likenesses appear in print. Fred Stimpson, president of the Bull Pen Hunting Club and host for the hunt, helped me assemble the hunters for the pictures. I explained to him that no more than four people should be in a photograph, and he agreed.

"Does it matter how many deer are in the picture?" he asked. I couldn't recall that Sharpley had ever laid down any rules limiting the game that could be photographed, so Fred Stimpson posed his friends against a line of a dozen or more antlered bucks hanging from their heels.

After the pictures were taken, I explained to my host about being stuck and having a broken fan belt, thanked him for his hospitality, and told him I was going back to the lodge and try to get help. "Don't worry," he said. "It is all being taken care of. You just stay right here with us."

Since I had so recently arrived and since he had just learned of my difficulties, I did not see how it was possible that everything was "all being taken care of," but I had no choice except to stay. I hoped to take a nap while the men hunted, but such was not to be. A gun was thrust into my hands and I was informed that I would occupy a stand during the afternoon drive. My protests were futile.

My stand (and that's exactly what it is—standing, standing, standing) was the next to the last one which meant that I had to walk nearly farther than anybody else. I had already trudged three miles over treacherous terrain, and my boots felt as if they weighed forty pounds each. I was exhausted.

Ben Morgan, director of the Alabama Department of Conservation, was assigned to occupy the stand with me. Maybe he volunteered, but I doubt it. He said to me in a firm voice, "When a deer comes, you are not to move a muscle or bat an eye until I tell you to shoot. If you make the slightest move, I will knock you down." He did not smile.

I chose that inopportune moment to be seized with a fit of coughing. My companion pounded me on the back, nearly depriving me of what little breath I had. "Don't let that happen again!" he warned.

Off in the distance I could hear the shouts of the drivers and the barking of the dogs moving toward us. Deer leaped past, their white tails held high, and turkeys scurried through the undergrowth, wild things frightened by the sounds of death and seeking safety in the deep woods. The deer and the turkeys were all out of range. Ben Morgan was disgusted. I was grateful.

About first dark, we congregated at the sub-camp, watched as seven dead bucks were loaded into a pick-up, climbed into vehicles ourselves, and returned to the lodge. Once again thoughts of home filled my mind, and once again Fred Stimpson told me not to fret. "We'll leave before long," he said.

Before departure time there were delays for:

1. Relaxing—this activity centered around the consumption of several bottles of fine whisky. I explained that I was already relaxed (limp from exhaustion was what I was) and needed only hot coffee.

2. Turkey calling contest—I also begged to be excused from this activity.

3. Shirttail cutting—a tribunal was empowered to try the cases of all hunters who had shot at a deer and missed. Convicted hunters had their shirttails cut off and tacked up on the wall along with the owner's name and date of the offense. A new rule was enacted that night to the effect that anyone who got stuck on the way to the lodge would lose a shirttail. It was a pretty pale green gabardine shirt.

4. Hollering contest—bets were made as to which of the drivers could yell the loudest, and a contest was held. Actu-

ally, what the men bet on was "whose nigger could holler the loudest." Judging proved to be difficult, and the finalists had to be listened to again and again. There was great dissatisfaction with the decision of the judges.

5. Supper—as fine and as welcome a meal as I ever ate.

6. Dividing the venison—each participant in the hunt (me included) was given a clean flour sack and sent outdoors in the damp cold. We stood in a circle with our eyes closed (apparently this aspect of the ritual was important) until called by name to step forward (eyes open then) to claim the meat. The meat was placed in the flour sack and the recipient returned to the circle to stand (eyes closed) until the distribution was complete.

7. Farewell.

I was to ride back to my car with Fred Stimpson. He, being the club president and the host, was naturally the last to leave. We walked over to his car and found that it had a flat tire. And an empty gas tank. Both were finally attended to.

By the time we reached my car, it had been pulled to higher, firmer ground, and one of the hunters, Count Darling (his real name), had fashioned a makeshift fan belt out of his necktie. The belt worked, but I had to drive very slowly. It was long, long after midnight before I got back to civilization.

My pictures turned out fine (I sent the governor, Fred Stimpson and Count Darling extra copies), and Vincent liked my story. He never did understand, though, why I was so tired.

Chapter 10

BIRMINGHAM was experiencing a post-war adjustment period along with the rest of the nation. Some people, the same ones who always referred to the war years as "the duration" spoke of this time as "after the duration."

Returning servicemen and -women needed jobs, and the *News* publicized this need for employment. The slogan was "Hire a Vet." Former employees of the *News* were returning and claiming their old jobs. Each returnee was welcomed and "mirated" over, and I finally met the people whose stories I had read and whose names I had heard.

As the veterans continued to return, I heard often in the newsroom, "When is Amasa coming back?" I knew about Amasa, though I had never met him. At every newspaper gathering, it seemed to me, Amasa stories were told. "Do you remember the time Amasa—?" or "Were you with us the night Amasa—?" and the stories started. I heard more about Amasa than I ever wanted to hear.

One night when I was out with Tommy Hill and he began on an Amasa recollection, I blurted out, "Tommy, if you mention that man's name one more time, I'll never go out with you again!"

I was working late one October night when the elevator door opened and out stepped a Navy lieutenant commander in his white dress uniform. Everybody in the newsroom shrieked, "Amasa!" and crowded around to embrace him and shake his hand and pat him on the back. Everybody except me. I kept on typing. I did stop long enough to give him a quick look. He was older than I had expected, not as tall and a bit overweight.

The commotion over his arrival grew as word spread to other floors that Amasa was back. A V-J Day celebration in miniature was going on right there in the newsroom. I kept on typing. I had already worked twelve hours that day, and I wanted to finish my story and go home. "You must be Kathryn," I heard a masculine voice say. Amasa had disengaged himself from his cluster of friends and was leaning on my desk. "I've heard about you."

"I've heard about you, too," I replied. I was tempted to add that I had heard too much, but I didn't.

"We're all going out to dinner to celebrate my homecoming. I'd like to take you with me," he said.

"Thank you, but I'm not the least bit interested."

Amasa turned away quickly, joined his entourage and they disappeared into the elevator. I kept on typing.

For three weeks he ignored me. Then one afternoon he sent a copy girl over with a note for me. "Would you be the least bit interested in going out to dinner with me tomorrow night?" it asked. Across the bottom I wrote, "I have nothing better to do," and the copy girl delivered my reply.

I don't remember where we went that night; maybe Joy Young's downtown. Nothing fancy. I do remember that we had a good time together. He talked some about his experiences on Okinawa where, he said, he was the only man more afraid of the rats ("they had big blue noses and long tusks") than he was of the Japs. He refused to get in a foxhole during Japanese air raids—that's where the rats with their blue noses and long tusks were, he said.

I remember, too, that we stayed out entirely too late. I had to be at work at seven o'clock in the morning. Amasa was on the *Age-Herald* staff. His hours were three o'clock in the afternoon to eleven o'clock at night.

A day or two later a copy girl delivered a note saying, "I'm off tomorrow night. Harry Lauder will be in town. Would you be the least bit interested in going with me to hear him sing?"

Sir Harry Lauder was seventy-five years old then and must have been on his final tour in the United States. He was more cautious than agile when he did a soft shoe across the stage, and his voice lacked the volume it had once had, but Sir Harry was still a master entertainer, and when he sang "I Wonder Who's Kissing Her Now" he got a standing ovation.

That night I learned that Amasa was something of an authority on vaudeville and musical comedy. Later I learned he not only had had leading roles in productions of the Birmingham Little Theatre but had also written plays for that group.

My next note from him said, "There's going to be a newspaper party Saturday night, a gathering of good friends. Would you be the least bit interested in going with me?"

At that party we danced to "It's Been A Long, Long Time" and "It Might As Well Be Spring." Vincent took my glasses off and hid them in the refrigerator. "You know what Dorothy Parker said: 'Men seldom make passes at girls who wear glasses,'" Vincent told me. Later Vincent claimed that his action was responsible for Amasa's falling in love with me. I always thought he fell in love with me the night I put on an apron and cooked supper for him.

I kept expecting him to send me a note asking, "Would you be the least bit interested in marrying me?" but he never did. In fact, he never did actually propose. Our friends assumed we were going to get married, but when Amasa quit his job and went to New York, they had doubts. They began to recall other times when he had nearly been led to the altar. He was forty years old.

"I've got to go to New York and find a good job. There's no future for me here on the *Age-Herald*," he told me. "I'll be back to get you."

Much later I learned that Amasa had been leaning up against the newspaper building one afternoon, chatting with some friends while they all waited to go to work, when Henry Vance came up. Henry was an older man, a newspaper columnist whom Amasa admired.

"Amasa," Henry said, "you were standing right in that same spot ten years ago. Will you be standing there ten years from now?" That's when Amasa decided to go to New York.

And he did come back to get me. We were married in the Methodist Church in Thomasville on February 10, 1946.

Cornelia Lively was my only attendant. Her husband, Bob, recently discharged from the Navy, helped Cousin Tabb decorate the church that Sunday afternoon before the wedding. They arranged tall candles against a background of smilax that my colored friend, Omah (he used to bring my Christmas trees when I was a child), brought from his woods. Osceola Green Hauge, my longtime friend, came from Pensacola to play the organ. Vincent was Amasa's best man.

When I walked down the aisle on my brother Wood's arm and saw how pale Amasa was and how frightened he looked, I was tempted to call the ceremony off. His voice was so weak that even I had difficulty hearing him repeat the vows, and I had to prompt him to look at me or to look at the minister at the proper times. I thought he would never get the ring on my finger.

As soon as we were outside the church, his color, his voice and his senses returned. "I never got married before," he said by way of explanation. In contrast to Amasa's fright, my own mother said I was flirtatious at the altar, chided me gently for my behavior.

We had quite a contingent of Birmingham friends at the wedding. We would have had many, many more if Bob Kincey, a *Birmingham News* columnist, had been able to carry out his plan. Bob wanted to hook two passenger cars to the back of a Birmingham-to-Mobile freight train and have the passenger cars taken off at Thomasville. He checked the schedule and found that the train would arrive in plenty of time for the wedding. Bob planned to have nearly everybody from the *News* and the *Age-Herald* on board.

Fortunately, wartime restrictions on railroad traffic were

still in effect, so, though he tried hard, Bob was unable to carry out his plan. I was vastly relieved. I had had nightmares about two carloads of convivial newspaper folks, with more than four hours to prime themselves for the event, pouring off that train on an up-to-that-time peaceful Sunday afternoon in Thomasville. I always meant to write a letter of thanks to the bureaucrat who denied Bob Kincey's request.

As Amasa and I were leaving the reception, Vincent called me aside and whispered, "If things don't work out, you can come back to work. I'll hold your job six months for you."

But it was twelve years before I wrote another news story.

Kitti was nine, Ben seven and Dilcy (her true name is Helen Ann) was three when Amasa died of a heart attack in 1956.

We were living in Selma where we had recently bought a home on Royal Street, a neighborhood of friendly families (there were thirty-three children in our block) within walking distance of an elementary school then under construction (I was the first PTA president at that new school—Edgewood), with a strip of woods behind the house for privacy and for play.

During the ten years of our marriage, I stayed at home with our children. I did all the traditional mother things: made hot dogs at PTA carnivals, baked cookies for school parties, taught a Sunday School class, and served on an assortment of committees—all for worthy causes.

I had good help with my projects and with my children. Viola Titus (her name was Viola Beverly then) came to work for me the week Amasa and I moved to Selma. She cleaned, washed, ironed and took care of the children, loving and petting and gently correcting each one. I don't know how I could have managed without Viola's help, especially during Amasa's long illness.

I continued to write. My typewriter usually stayed on the end of the dining room table or on the kitchen counter. *Inn Dixie,* a magazine distributed by the Dinkler Hotel chain, bought character sketches I wrote, and *The Progressive Farmer* was also a good market. The *Birmingham News Magazine,* a Sunday supplement that carried area features, used nearly everything I sent them.

For sixteen years (1950–1966), I wrote a column called "Around Our House" which was run in weekly papers throughout the state. Most of the columns began with something humorous the children had done or said, and each column contained practical household hints plus a favorite recipe.

I identified the children by ages, not by names, which served to protect their privacy while at the same time letting readers know what stages they were passing through. Those columns, some neatly preserved in scrapbooks but most stuffed into boxes, are excellent reminders of the three Windhams' growing-up-years—if I ever get them arranged chronologically.

I don't believe the children ever knew I was writing about them (it was no secret—we just never discussed it), and I'm not sure one of them has ever read the old columns, not even the ones in the scrapbooks.

It was not until Dilcy entered first grade that I returned to newspapering. The children, having lost a loving father who kissed them good night and then was gone forever when they waked up the next morning, needed the security of having a mother at home.

My work at the *Selma Times-Journal* was on a part-time basis with the understanding that I would be at home every afternoon when the children got out of school. I also had school holidays and vacations off—without pay, of course. It seems in retrospect a very loose employment arrangement I had, but it suited the *Times-Journal* and me: I wanted to be back in the news-gathering business, and the paper needed someone with my journalistic background. Our relationship lasted nearly fourteen years.

Chapter 11

I DON'T think I ever had an official title at the *Times-Journal*, so I called myself whatever fit the occasion: state editor, women's news editor, sports writer, political reporter, feature writer, even assistant editor. And I still handled Odd-Egg Editor assignments, many of them.

Arthur Capell was city editor, James Wallace was managing editor and Sam Ezell wrote sports much of the time I was at the paper. Their duties and titles also were subject to change.

Our reference library was a long white wall down one side of the newsroom on which we wrote such bits of information as the height of the Alabama River during bad floods, dates of record high and low temperatures, vote totals in elections, football scores, traffic fatalities by months and years, sizes of champion watermelons and turnips (my department), dates of the opening of the first cotton bloom and ginning of the first bale, and telephone numbers, of course.

On that wall were also written funny mistakes in the paper, and a count of the words in Mrs. Octavia S. Wynn's sentences. Mrs. Wynn was a pioneer newspaper woman in Selma who was noted for her long, involved sentences. As I recall, her record was a sentence 147 words long. The *Times-Journal* lost its reference library when new owners covered the wall with paint and plywood paneling. Some of Selma's history, bits of trivia nowhere else recorded, vanished forever.

One of Selma's worst floods, duly recorded on that wall, came in the spring of 1961. Protracted rains sent the Alabama River out of its banks to depths greater than any witnesses could remember. As the waters continued to rise, families by the hundreds were evacuated from low-lying areas in Selmont, Blackwell's Bend, Meredith's Landing and other points along the river and brought to Selma. Operators of motor boats and skiffs worked day and night in the cold rain rescuing stranded people from barns, small islands, roof tops, even trees.

In Selma a volunteer army of housewives, businessmen, high school students, clergy and others manned a registration center at the National Guard Armory, distributed food and clothing and arranged for temporary shelter for the evacuees. The local workers had been on the job for three days or more and were all very tired. As if by magic, a group of professional Red Cross workers from Boston arrived at the armory. They wore crisp, fresh uniforms and had a supply of well-sharpened pencils.

I was in the midst of interviewing an elderly black man when one of the professionals dismissed me. "You may go now. I'll take over," she said.

I gave her my chair, but I did not move far away. I

listened as she tried to continue the interview. There was a very wide communication gap between her proper Bostonian English and his Alabama Black Belt dialect. She tried hard, and he was as patient and polite as could be. Finally she turned to me in desperation and exclaimed, "I can't understand a word he is saying!" And the elderly man turned to me to ask, "Miss, what she say?"

The Red Cross lady gave me her chair and stood beside me to listen and to learn.

"How deep was the water in your house when you left?" I asked. It was one of the questions on a printed form.

"Well, Miss, when I lef' hit were titty high."

I'm certain the proper Bostonian did not understand that answer!

It was during that same disaster that I, trying to establish rapport and to make the man I was interviewing feel more at ease, invoked the name of my friend Catherine Revel. Catherine had worked with the Welfare Department for years and was well known and loved throughout the county.

"You know Mrs. Revel, don't you?" I asked.

The man's face brightened. "Oh, yes, ma'am, I knows Miz Revel well. I don't hardly see how we could have had this flood without her!"

Nobody laughed harder over that story than Catherine Revel did.

The *Times-Journal* covered the story of that flood from the first warnings that the river would rise until the refugees were able to return to whatever was left of their homes. Some of that coverage was devoted to the heroism of the men in their small boats, men who maneuvered their crafts through swift, debris-filled currents to rescue black families whom they had never seen before and whom they would likely never see again.

It was some of these same men who, a few years later, rode with Sheriff Jim Clark's mounted posse, swinging billy clubs with the same sense of righteousness that had spurred them to risk their lives in an angry river.

That time of the posse, the marches, the demonstrations, that time from the early summer of 1963 until late spring of 1965 was a strange, confused time in Selma. And though I was an observer, as a newspaper reporter, of much of the activity, it is hard for me to sort out my memories.

I recall passing the Tabernacle Baptist Church, on Broad Street a few blocks from my home, one night in June, 1963, and finding the area ringed with helmeted officers standing shoulder to shoulder. Inside the church, a mass meeting of some 350 persons, nearly all blacks, was being held. It was the first of many such meetings designed to unite the black community in an effort to achieve full rights of citizenship.

I pulled over to the curb and sat in my car watching the cordon of men with their billy clubs, listening to the singing coming from the church, and wondering what it all meant, where it would lead.

Later I heard those songs and others as, day after day, groups of protestors marched from Brown Chapel to the Dallas County courthouse. I stood on the sidewalk with my camera, a Yashica, to take pictures for the paper "in case anything happens."

The processions were peaceful. The marchers followed the instructions of Wilson Baker, Selma's public safety director, to march four abreast and to avoid disrupting traffic. There were occasional clusters of spectators along the sidewalks, and other people watched from the upstairs windows of stores (especially Tepper's) along the route.

One of the daily watchers from Tepper's windows commented to me, "I laugh every time I see some of the marchers stop singing, nod to you and say, 'Good morning, Mrs. Windham.'" I did have a good many nodding acquaintances among the marchers. And, as a result of my daily exposure to the singing, I was the only white person in my circle of friends who knew all the verses of all the freedom songs.

Sometimes I would follow the marchers around to the courthouse and watch as they lined up on the sidewalk waiting to get into the voting registrar's office or protesting the fact that the office was closed.

Occasionally I'd catch a glimpse of Circuit Judge James Hare standing in an upstairs window at the courthouse looking down at the crowd, and I knew he was mentally categorizing them, picking out the physical characteristics that marked different African tribes: "There're two Ibos. There's a Bantu. And the one over there looks like a Watusi." It was generally believed that Sheriff Clark took his orders from Judge Hare. At least the sheriff's actions were influenced by what Judge Hare thought should be done.

I watched Sheriff Clark and his deputies walk up and down the long line of people standing outside the courthouse, ordering them to stand single file, to leave space on the sidewalks for "persons who need to enter the courthouse on legitimate business." Leaders of the demonstrations called the actions of the sheriff and his deputies harrassment, and resentment against them grew.

One morning as I stood on the landing outside the courthouse waiting for "something big to happen," it did.

I heard a commotion in the line and turned in time to see a large black woman grab Sheriff Clark as he walked by, snatch his billy club and throw him to the ground. Two deputies came instantly to the sheriff's rescue before any blows were struck, and it took the three of them to subdue the irate woman and wrest the baton from her. I took a picture of the struggle.

My picture, as were other photographs taken at the scene, was misleading. It showed the woman being held on the ground by the two deputies while the sheriff appeared to be about to strike her with the club. Such was not the case: the sheriff was attempting to retrieve the weapon from the woman's grasp. I heard later, though I never verified it, that the woman was a bouncer in a black night spot.

I tried to make clear what actually happened at the Dallas County courthouse that morning. It may have been the only time I ever defended Sheriff Jim Clark.

I wish I had kept a diary or journal during that period, but I didn't, so my memories are in bits and snippets, and thinking back is like coming upon a batch of unidentified negatives and holding each one up to the light.

There was the afternoon when Sheriff Clark and his forces herded more than 100 school children, all of them absent from classes to take part in the mass demonstrations, from the courthouse, through downtown Salem, down Mulberry Street and out into the countryside. It was no slow, leisurely procession: the groups alternatively ran and walked as the sheriff directed the action from his slow-moving automobile.

The arrests were made on charges of truancy, the sheriff

said, and, since the jails were full, it was his intention to march the students out to the Fraternal Order of Police Lodge, some six miles from the courthouse, where they were to be held until their cases were disposed of. About halfway to their destination, the students broke ranks and fled into the homes of black families and into wooded areas along the route. The law enforcement officers did not give chase.

This forced march ("They wanted to march, so we arranged a good one for them") prompted Roswell Falkenberry, editor of the *Selma Times-Journal*, to write a front page editorial critical of the sheriff's actions. The editorial also denounced the continuing street demonstrations, declaring, "The play-acting by all persons concerned must stop."

The account of the sheriff-sponsored march by the students created a surge of indignation in the conservative white community. One of my friends, as well known and respected for her sharp mind as for her elegant manners, was so incensed by the incident that she went to the courthouse to vent her outrage personally on the sheriff. She wore her hat and gloves for the occasion.

She was ushered into the sheriff's office where she fell immediate victim to Jim Clark's charisma. So charmed was she by his gracious manners and by his justification of his actions that her anger melted away and she heard herself asking politely, "How are Mrs. Clark and your children?"

Then there was the occasion two days after the involuntary trek by the students, when hundreds of youths, many of whom had been on that excursion, joined adults in a prayer service outside the courthouse. They knelt to pray for Sheriff Jim Clark's prompt recovery. The sheriff had been hospitalized for observation following his complaints of severe chest pains. The prayers were answered.

As the demonstrations continued, more and more newsmen, more and more television cameramen came into Selma to write about and photograph the events. Reporters from New York and Washington were commonplace. Every now and then I found myself standing beside a newsman from London or from Frankfort on the Main or from Brisbane. No matter where they came from, those newsmen all asked the same kinds of questions.

The evening newscasts on all networks featured scenes from Selma, marches, rallies, confrontations. And nearly every night after the early evening news, my mother would call from Thomasville. "Are you and the children all right? Are you safe?" She needed reassurance. I think she would have liked for us to come refugee in Thomasville. During each call, I assured Mother of our well-being, tried to ease her fears about the possibilities of riots and destruction and violence.

Actually, our lives went on at a normal routine, almost unaffected by the events downtown. Kitti was a senior in high school, Ben was in the eleventh grade, and Dilcy was in junior high school, all enrolled at Albert G. Parrish High School, only a few blocks away. In the afternoons they came home, as they always had, unless they had band practice or play rehearsals, or Scouts or Methodist Youth Fellowship meetings or art lessons or such. They had never gone downtown to hang out after school, and there was certainly no reason for them to start then. As students at Parrish, their classes and extra-curricular activities continued without disruption.

Over at Richard B. Hudson High School, across Summerfield Road, daily absences ran between 800–900 students as the demonstrations moved toward a climax.

The children and I watched the news reports on television, and I told them what I had seen and heard downtown during the day. We talked about the rumors they had heard at school, but we talked about other topics, too.

Viola came to work every day. She had been with me nearly nineteen years then, but I did not know what she thought about the turmoil, what was going on in her mind. One morning when I went to pick her up and she started to open the back door of the car, I asked, "Viola, don't you want to sit up here by me?"

"No'm," she replied. "I been riding on the back seat all this time, I'll just keep on." She slammed the door. "'Scuse me. Didn't mean to raise such a racket."

When I covered the memorial services for Jimmy Lee Jackson, a twenty-six-year-old black man who was shot by a state trooper during a nighttime demonstration in nearby Marion, I saw Viola in the throng that crowded in and around Brown Chapel. She was dressed finer than I had ever seen her dressed before. Our eyes met briefly, but neither of us spoke. And we never mentioned the incident.

Never once during those tense weeks did I feel uneasy for my own safety. The most direct route from the *Times-Journal* to my home ran through the heart of a black area. It was the route I had always used to go home, so I continued to use it, even at night, though it was poorly lighted and not heavily traveled. I was never afraid.

On only one occasion was I ever frightened, and then my fear was for the safety of my son, Ben. I let Ben go to town with me one afternoon to take pictures of a well-publicized march. I expected that there would be trouble, so I don't know why I took the risk of letting Ben be downtown. He should have stayed at home that March Saturday. Both of us should have.

The Reverend Joseph Ellwanger, pastor of a white Lutheran congregation in Birmingham, announced early in the week that he was bringing a group of ministers, teachers and other professional people to Selma to march in support of the blacks. His group, some seventy strong, was known as the Concerned White Citizens of Alabama.

Opposition to the proposed march spread rapidly through the white community. It was upsetting enough to have white protestors come from distant states, but it was almost unthinkable that a group of white people would come from a neighboring city (and didn't they have enough problems there crying out for their concern?) to join ranks with the blacks. Furthermore, Joseph Ellwanger had close ties to Selma: his father had been pastor of the Lutheran Church here, and Joseph himself had spent some of his growing-up years in Selma.

Efforts were made to persuade Joseph to cancel the march. I called him, as did other Selma acquaintances, to plead with him not to come. I outlined for him the potentially explosive situation in Selma and I warned him of the violent hatred that was focusing on his group. I added that the proposed display of public piety was stupid, dangerous and unwelcome.

Joseph seemed distressed that there should be opposition to their show of concern—distressed but not deterred. "We must make a public expression of our concern for the rights of our brothers," he told me.

So Saturday afternoon, March 5, when all the cameras

were in place, the Concerned White Citizens of Alabama emerged from the basement of a black church on Jeff Davis Avenue and began their trek to town. Leading the way was the gaunt, concerned minister. Down the sidewalks where he had played as a boy he led his flock. They walked in groups of four so as not to violate the city's parade ordinance, and each group had a leader with his badge of authority, a yellow triangle of cloth, pinned to his lapel. There was no police escort.

The march started peacefully enough, but after a few blocks motorists began driving slowly beside the marchers and shouting obscenities at them. By the time they reached the courthouse, a large and hostile reception committee was waiting. The mood was ugly. Joseph Ellwanger's efforts to speak were drowned out by catcalls and jeers. A placard-carrier (his sign read "Silence Is No Longer Golden") was hit and shoved to the ground.

Across the street, three white men drove up in an old model car. One of them jumped out, raised the hood and poured a liquid into the carburetor. The driver raced the motor. A heavy cloud of black smoke engulfed the demonstrators and the hecklers. A cluster of young blacks standing nearby laughed at the spectacle.

Photographers trying to take pictures of the scene were shoved roughly aside. One of them was knocked to the pavement. Blood oozed from a wound on the back of his head.

"Kill them! Kill them!" shouted a chorus of angry white women standing near me. They waved clenched fists in the air, and the veins in their necks stood out like taut pink cords. "Kill them! Kill them!"

I suddenly realized that Ben was not with me. We had become separated. I was frantic. Ben had a camera hanging around his neck. He was a perfect target for some hate-filled member of that screaming mob.

I don't know how long it took me to find him. It seemed forever. I pushed through the crowd, saw the contempt and hatred on their faces, as I searched the smoke-filled street for my son. It may have been the pall of smoke that saved him from being beaten.

I spied him across the street talking with one of his friends. "I need the camera," I told him. I didn't want him to know how frightened I had been. By then the taunting, cursing mob had surrounded the CWCA delegation. I wondered if I dared take my camera from around my neck.

Just then Selma's Public Safety Director Wilson Baker, big, fearless, authoritative Wilson Baker, pushed his way through the mob and ordered them to disperse at once. Few people, black or white, disobeyed Wilson Baker's orders. Sheriff's deputies appeared suddenly (it was rumored that they had been watching from the courthouse and had come out only when it appeared the situation was about to get completely out of control) and escorted Joseph and his followers to safety.

That Saturday afternoon outside the Dallas County Courthouse was the only time during those tense weeks of demonstrations that I was ever afraid. I was angry many times and discouraged and frustrated, but never afraid.

Some of my anger and frustration centered on my own church, Church Street Methodist. As early efforts were underway to integrate local restaurants, drug store lunch counters and soda fountains ("Don't Buy Where You Can't Eat"), picture shows and hotels, a group of men at our church organized a patrol to "keep the niggers out."

As the Sunday morning worship hours approached, some of these self-proclaimed protectors stationed themselves at the entrances to the church and others paced back and forth on the sidewalks, ever on the alert for any dark-skinned person who might try to join in the worship services. They even screened white-skinned visitors whose backgrounds and motives might be questionable.

The presence of these men was intimidating, and there were few efforts made to integrate the services. There was, on one occasion, some pushing and shoving of a black man to convince him that he was not welcome.

That episode moved me to action. I called first the chairman of the board of stewards to protest what I considered both unwise and unchristian behavior by representatives of our church. I got a long lecture about the proud history of that white congregation. Then I called the minister who chuckled and said, "Well, the method has been effective—it has kept them out!"

The Church Street Methodist Church was not the only house of worship in Selma that used guardians to discourage unwanted visitors. The practice was rather widespread.

On a late September Sunday in 1963, the First Presbyterian Church (the downtown brick church with the city clock in its bell tower) was quietly integrated by a small group of young black girls who were courteously ushered to seats in an empty balcony.

Soon afterwards a member of that church wrote an open letter to those young people, a letter that was published in the *Selma Times-Journal*. The lengthy letter ended: "You integrated the First Presbyterian Church of Selma, Alabama? Little girls, we don't even integrate with many white people. If you came to our church for a hundred years, sat in the servants' balcony, or even with the congregation, ninety-eight percent of the ladies and gentlemen of this church would never look around, stir or even move a muscle. We would not reject you; we would not accept you; we would simply look around you, over you, through you and freeze you numb."

The little group never paid a return visit to the Presbyterian Church.

I was at my own church, attending a district rally that afternoon of March 7 (Sunday), the day that became known as Bloody Sunday. Bishop Kenneth Goodson addressed the gathering. Nobody inside the sanctuary was aware of the brutal confrontation taking place between the civil rights marchers and the members of the sheriff's mounted posse and the state troopers on a graceful river bridge not five blocks away.

If I had not been at that church meeting, I might have watched from the *Times-Journal* building as mounted posse members chased blacks back across the bridge, back to havens around Brown Chapel; might have heard the frightened cries and the shouted oaths; might have seen hapless victims whacked with billy clubs; might have choked and gagged on the tear gas.

But I was safe, safe inside my church. I watched that sad, senseless drama on the television newscasts that night, and I must have seen two dozen replays of it since. Somehow that bridge, Edmund Pettus Bridge, named to honor a

Confederate hero, has become the symbol of Selma, has become one of the nation's best-known landmarks.

I wasn't there that Sunday, but I see the bridge each time I go downtown. And I remember.

Selma's schools, too, were victims of the racial turmoil. The schools were still segregated then: white students attended Albert G. Parrish High School, and black students were enrolled at Richard B. Hudson High School. Elementary schools were also racially segregated. The day of the private academy had not yet arrived.

Monday morning, the Monday after Bloody Sunday, there were 709 students absent from Hudson High School, nearly half of the student body. Normally the absences among the 1,444 students were seventy-five to eighty per day, but 1965 was not a normal time.

Hudson High had its largest number of absences, 1,120, on March 15, when a memorial service was held for the Rev. James Reeb. The Rev. Mr. Reeb, a white minister from out of state, died after he was assaulted on a Selma street. His death was the only fatality in Selma during the months of demonstrations.

I was interested in the pattern of absences from the black schools (elementary schools also had more absences than usual during the period) not only as a reporter but also a member of the Selma City School Board. State allotments of funds for the operation of schools were based on average daily attendance. I never quite understood the formula, but I did understand that the absences were costing the school system thousands of dollars.

Dr. Austin R. Meadows, state superintendent of education, released a statement reminding parents that all children sixteen years of age and under who had not graduated from high school were required by Alabama law to attend school regularly. Parents whose children failed to attend school were guilty of a misdemeanor and, upon conviction, subject to a fine of not more than $100 and hard labor for the county for not more than ninety days.

Dr. Meadows must have known, as members of the school board knew and as truant students knew and as demonstration leaders who encouraged truancy knew, that there were not enough law enforcement personnel in Selma to arrest erring parents and no place to jail them if they were arrested.

Probate Judge Bernard Reynolds, who acted as juvenile court judge, had a backlog of hundreds of cases of school children, most of them taken into custody by Sheriff Clark. It was Judge Reynolds's strategy to give the first offenders a stern lecture and release them to the custody of reliable family members, who were also given a lecture. The judge just didn't have time to deliver all the lectures needed. (Incidentally, it was Judge Reynolds who removed the "White" and "Colored" signs over the drinking fountains in the courthouse. He pointed to that action as evidence of his moderate racial stance.)

At our school board meetings we had lengthy discussions about how to deal with the truants. Expelling them would be counterproductive: we wanted them in school, learning. They must be penalized for missing classes, we agreed, but they should be offered an opportunity to make up the work. I don't recall how many seniors failed to graduate at Hudson High School that year.

Truancy was a minor problem compared with the problem the board faced in carrying out the federal court orders to desegregate (we were told that the word "desegregate" caused less angry resistance than the word "integrate") the schools.

Locally there was bitter opposition to any efforts to comply with the federal guidelines for desegregation, and this opposition was encouraged and reinforced by Governor George Wallace. I wish I had kept an orderly record of dates and events so that I would know in what sequence and time frame certain actions took place. I recall being summoned to Montgomery to meet with Governor Wallace on two occasions. The first time was a large gathering of school board members and superintendents from throughout the state who were "advised" not to sign any agreement to comply with the federal regulations.

Later, Edgar Stewart, then chairman of the Selma City School Board, and I (I'm not sure why I was chosen unless I happened to be the only board member available to go to Montgomery on short notice) were summoned for a semi-private meeting with the governor. He had been informed that the Selma board would likely sign the letter of compliance and would begin the process of desegregating the public schools, and he wanted the board to be fully aware of the potential dangers of such action.

"I cannot be responsible for what might happen in Selma," he warned us. There were implications that the Ku Klux Klan, National States Rights Party and other such radical groups, groups which the governor said had been held in check, might be expected to concentrate their anger on Selma if steps were taken to integrate (his word) the schools there.

The Selma City School Board did sign the agreement to follow the court-ordered guidelines for desegregation. It was the law, and though we may have had misgivings, we were law-abiding citizens and believed that the majority of Selmians would understand and accept our actions.

There were repercussions.

Mass meetings of concerned citizens ("concern" was a much-used word during that period) were called to denounce the action of the school board and of its members, and to formulate plans for insuring that there would be no mixing of the races.

At one of those meetings, Mayor Joe Smitherman called me a "cornfield intellectual." I was present at that meeting, and he pointed straight at me. He thought I would be angry, but I was delighted. Nobody had ever called me an intellectual of any kind. The next morning I had a florist deliver an arrangement of dried ears of corn to the mayor's office. There was no card with the gift. The mayor kept that display in his office for many months. I think the weevils finally ate it.

Other incidents were less pleasant: an after-midnight telephone call with heavy breathing on the line; a scattering of hate mail; snubs from former friends.

Then one night, very late, we left a school board meeting, walked to the parking area, and found the windshields of our cars has been shot. I drove my car with its cracked windshield for many weeks before I had it replaced. I hoped whoever had fired the shot would see the car and be reminded of a cowardly act.

Our plans for desegregation moved forward. We had strong support from the *Selma Times-Journal* where Editor Roswell Falkenberry used the news columns to keep the public informed and used the editorial columns to urge calm acceptance of the law.

Fortunately, our school superintendent, Joseph A. Pickard, was a meticulous planner. He issued clear, concise instructions to principals and faculty members; he made talks to civic clubs and school groups; and he conferred often with officials in city government to make certain that pupils and teachers would be safe.

Selma's plan for desegregation called for freedom of choice for students in grades one through four the first year, 1965–66.

On September 3, 1965, six neatly dressed little black girls were enrolled at Frances Thomas School. Their eight-thirty arrival, which was without incident, ended segregation in Selma's public schools.

Later in the morning, small groups of black students were enrolled at formerly all-white Baker and Edgewood schools. No bystanders were allowed at any of the schools, and members of the news media had been requested in advance to refrain from entering the school areas. Press facilities were provided in the Board of Education building, but only one out-of-town newsman appeared. My story of the events of that day was headlined: "Schools Integrate Quietly In Selma." It was one of the most welcome headlines I ever read.

John Tyler Morgan Academy, the city's newly organized private school, opened the following week. It is ironic that this private academy should be named for a Confederate hero who is quoted as saying, "As for me and my family, it will be the public school."

Five years later, in July, 1970, Selma had its first black

school board members. Mrs. Mary Coleman, who lived in a rented house near the railroad tracks on Lavender Street, and the Rev. P. H. Lewis, pastor of Brown Chapel, were chosen to fill vacancies on the board. The Selma School Board was a self-perpetuating body, said to be the only one of its kind in the United States. The Rev. Mr. Lewis was transferred to an out-of-town church after he had served on the board only four months. Mrs. Coleman served two years, resigning her position when she moved her family to Huntsville.

I came to know Mrs. Coleman when I would ride her home at night after our board meetings. She had no automobile, and I suppose both she and the white male members of the board would have been uncomfortable if any of them had taken her home, so she and I rode together. I don't recall that there was ever any discussion of these transportation arrangements—certainly Mrs. Coleman never asked me to take her home—but it seemed a natural courtesy. She and I had many common concerns (that word again!) and conversation came easily.

The two black members of the board were appointed the same year that Selma's high schools were desegregated. Albert G. Parrish High School and Richard B. Hudson High School were combined to form Selma High School. Minor but disturbing incidents accompanied that desegregation. Vandals defaced the new sign in front of the school, and they chopped down several of the trees that lined the median at the entrance to the campus. The paint was removed from the sign, and the downed trees were replanted. Those events seem so long ago, almost a part of another lifetime. Recently I came across a batch of notes taken at hearings, meetings and trials during those uneasy years of the 1960s. The notes are not dated, but they contain the names of individuals who left enduring reminders of their presence in Selma:

John Doar, tall, lanky Justice Department lawyer representing a Selma University student who was arrested across from the courthouse. The same student testified that Dr. D. C. Owens, president of Selma University, would not allow SNCL organizers to come on the campus;

Blanchard McLeod, circuit solicitor, who told of having a highway patrol escort from Selma to his home in Camden;

Judge Bernard Reynolds, Probate Judge, who was questioned about his handling of juvenile cases and who, during his discussion of the tense situation in July, 1964, testified he "would not let my wife and teen-age daughters visit friends in North Selma because they would have to pass through the colored section";

McLean Pitts, Selma attorney, matching wits with John Doar;

John Lewis, "outside agitator" (now a member of Congress), arrested at the Thirsty Boy, a downtown Selma fast food establishment;

The Rev. L. L. Anderson, Hosea Williams, Amelia Boynton, Frederick Reese, James Gildersleeve, Judge Brevard Hand, the Rev. Claude Brown, Judge Hugh Mallory, Judge Daniel Thomas—their names are scattered through my disorganized notes.

There are notes taken during the testimony of Judge Hare, on what occasion I do not know, who identified himself as associate judge of the Fourth Judicial Court and who told of receiving information relative to a contemplated drop into Selma by members of the 101st Airborne Division in September of 1963 to help quell anticipated "trouble."

He told also of seeing a TV truck parked near the courthouse and another parked across the street. Upon inquiring why the television crews were present, Judge Hare said he was told, "We damn sure haven't come from Atlanta to tape someone walking with a sign. All hell is supposed to bust loose in the next hour's time."

The paratroopers never came nor did all hell break loose, not at that time.

There are also notes from Federal Judge Daniel Thomas's direction for handling the long lines of people who were attempting to register to vote. Numbers were to be passed out to the first 100 persons in line, the judge ordered, and the line was to be formed at the Lauderdale Street entrance to the courthouse.

His order, the judge said, should end the "senseless discussion of which is the front door of the courthouse." There had been sharp disagreement, even marches, over whether the front door of the courthouse was on Lauderdale Street or on Alabama Avenue. The demonstrators had declared one entrance to be the front door, and Sheriff Clark and his adherents had chosen the other. The squabbling went on for days.

Judge Thomas's angry denunciation of the "senseless discussion" could well have applied to other issues associated with that period of upheaval.

One of my clearest memories of those months is of a rainy day when Selma Mayor Joe Smitherman stood beneath an umbrella at a police barricade near Brown Chapel.

He was a young man, thirty-five years old. He was skinny, had short hair, almost a crew cut, and his ears stuck out. He had been mayor only a few months.

He stood motionless, the rain dropping off his black umbrella, gazing at the hundreds and hundreds of protestors milling about on the other side of the barricade. His stance, his expression, even the background of dark clouds bespoke bafflement and dejection.

I remember watching him and thinking, "Joe will never survive—he can't cope with this adversity."

But he did survive and he did cope. Twenty-five years later he is still mayor.

I remember Joe on happier occasions when he would come into the newspaper office to bring a news item or to visit and, while he was talking to me, would suddenly leap flat-footed up onto my desk.

I don't believe he can still perform that athletic feat!

Usually when Joe came to the *Times-Journal* it was to talk to his friend Arthur Capell. Arthur should have won a Pulitzer Prize for his day-to-day coverage of the civil rights movement in Selma. Through all those months of bitterness and distrust, Arthur kept the respect and the confidence of the white community and the black community. They knew what he said and what he wrote were true.

Out-of-town journalists sought Arthur out. They depended on him heavily for background information and for access to news sources. A few if them even used Arthur's coverage of events, with minor changes, and sent the stories to their papers with their own by-lines.

It never seemed to upset Arthur that his reporting was ignored by the selectors-of-award winners. I think he knew, deep in his heart, that he and Wilson Baker and a handful of other folks had held Selma together in perilous times. Not even a Pulitzer Prize could equal that knowledge.

Selma's trials did not end with the departure of the "outside agitators." Most of those men and women, drawn to Selma by motives still undefined for some of them, packed their suitcases and their knapsacks and left after the Selma-to-Montgomery march.

In my travels, I often meet people who, when they learn I am from Selma, say proudly, "I was there. I marched in Selma." They say it in reverent tones, as though they expect a star in their crowns for each step they took. When I ask, "Have you been back since?" they seem surprised and a bit embarrassed by the question. Sometimes I add, "If you have not been back, it indicates to me that you really don't give a damn what happened to Selma." The former marchers do not always react kindly.

Selma was forever changed by the events of the 1960s. Changes, many long overdue, came in its political alignments, in its business community, in its social life, even in its churches. The First Presbyterian Church, temporarily integrated by teen-age black girls so long ago, now hosts a citywide performance of Handel's *Messiah* each December with members of both races singing and listening. And when the Stillman College choir came to sing at that church, there was hardly standing room for the people, both black and white, who crowded into the sanctuary to hear them.

Even the city's landscape has changed. The grand old Hotel Albert, patterned after the Doge's Palace in Venice, was razed in 1968. The City Hall now stands on its site. And down the street the Wilby Theatre, on whose stage minstrels and operas and plays direct from New York were performed, burned on a June afternoon in 1972. The fire started at a matinee performance of *Mary, Queen of Scots,* and the spectators at that movie never got to see Vanessa Redgrave's head lopped off.

My life was changing too. The two oldest children had graduated from college, and the youngest was a student at the University of Montevallo. The newspaper was sold to an out-of-town chain, and I knew the new owners would not be as accepting of my unorthodox working habits as my longtime employers had been. I wasn't at all sure I could learn to write on a computer—or that I wanted to.

It was time for me to leave the newspaper business. So I did.

Old habits are hard to break though. I still find myself wanting to ask people questions that are none of my business, just as I did for years as a reporter. And I still miss knowing the behind-the-scenes parts of stories, the interesting intrigues and sidelights that never get into print.

And I haven't seen an odd egg in a long, long time.

Printed in the United States
128161LV00004B/252/A